TEN NOVEMBER

A Play by Steven Dietz

Music and Lyrics by Eric Bain Peltoniemi

No part of this book may be reproduced, stored in a retrieval system, or transmitted in any form, by any means, including mechanical, electronic, photocopying, recording, or otherwise, without the prior written permission of the publisher.

SAMUEL FRENCH, INC.
45 WEST 25th STREET NEW YORK 10010
7623 SUNSET BOULEVARD HOLLYWOOD 90046
LONDON TORONTO

Book Copyright © 1987, 1988 by Steven John Dietz
"Fare-Thee-Well" Copyright © 1987, 1988 by Steven John Dietz
All other Lyrics Copyright © 1987, 1988 by Eric Bain Peltoniemi

ALL RIGHTS RESERVED

Amateurs wishing to arrange for the production of TEN NOVEMBER must make application to SAMUEL FRENCH, INC., at 45 West 25th Street, New York, NY 10010, giving the following particulars:

(1) The name of the town and theatre or hall of the proposed production will be presented.
(2) The maximum seating capacity of the theatre or hall.
(3) Scale of ticket prices.
(4) The number of performances intended and the dates thereof.
(5) Indicate whether you will use an orchestration or simply a piano.

Upon receipt of these particulars SAMUEL FRENCH, INC., will quote terms and availability.
Stock royalty quoted on application to SAMUEL FRENCH, INC., 45 West 25th Street, New York, NY 10010.
For all other rights than those stipulated above, apply to International Creative Management, Inc., 40 West 57th Street, New York, NY 10019.

2 Guitar/Bass scores

will be loaned two months prior to the production ONLY on receipt of the royalty quoted for all performances, the rental fee and a refundable deposit. The deposit will be refunded on the safe return to SAMUEL FRENCH, INC. of all materials loaned for the production.

Anyone presenting the play shall not commit or authorize any act of omission by which the copyright of the play or the right to copyright same may be impaired.
No changes shall be made in the play for the purpose of your production unless authorized in writing.
The publication of this play does not imply that it is necessarily available for performance by amateurs or professionals. Amateurs and professionals considering a production are strongly advised in their own interests to apply to Samuel French, Inc., for consent before starting rehearsals, advertising, or booking a theatre or hall.

Printed in the U.S.A.

ISBN 0 573 69183 5

IMPORTANT BILLING AND CREDIT REQUIREMENTS

All producers of TEN NOVEMBER *must* give credit to the Authors of the Work in all programs distributed in connection with performances of the Work, and in all instances in which the title of the Work appears for the purposes of advertising, publicizing or otherwise exploiting a production thereof; including, without limitation to, programs, souvenir books and playbills. The names of the Authors *must* also appear on a separate line in which no other matter appears, immediately following the title of the Work, and *must* be in size of type not less than 50% of the size of type used for the title of the Work. Billing *must* be substantially as follows:

(Name of Producer)

presents

TEN NOVEMBER

A Play by	Music and Lyrics by
Steven Dietz	Eric Bain Peltoniemi

    The playwright wishes to thank Michael Miner for arranging this "shotgun marriage" with Mr. Peltoniemi, the Playwrights' Center, Minneapolis, for their support, and dramaturg Steven E. Alter for his relentless curiousity.

    The composer/lyricist wishes to acknowledge Leslie Ball, Prudence Johnson, Ruth MacKenzie and Jeffrey Willkomm, whose talents greatly inspired the score, and Dr. Jean-Michel Delile of Bordeaux for being *le oeil de Dieu* overlooking his Gallic poetization.

Wisdom Bridge Theatre premiered *Ten November* from September 9 through November 1, 1987. Richard E.T. White directed. Set and lighting were designed by Michael S. Philippi, costumes by Jessica Hahn, special projection effects by John Boesche and sound by Rob Milburn. The cast was as follows:

ACTOR ONE	Danny Goldring
ACTOR TWO	Juan Ramirez
ACTOR THREE	Harry J. Lennix
ACTOR FOUR	Vince Viverito, Sr.
ACTOR FIVE	Larry Brandenburg
ACTOR SIX	Edward Wilkerson, Jr.
ACTOR SEVEN	William Dick
ACTOR EIGHT	Joe Van Slyke
ACTOR NINE	Robert Bundy
SINGERS	Ora Jones, Valarie Tekosky, Nancy Voights
MUSICIANS	David Onderdonk, Stuart Rosenberg

The play was subsequently produced at Actors Theatre of St. Paul, from October 30 through November 28, 1987 and was brought back for a further run from February 26 through March 19, 1988. Steven Dietz directed. The set was designed by Lori Lynne Sullivan, costumes by Sandra Nei Schulte and lighting by Nayna Ramey. The cast was as follows:

ACTOR ONE	Louis Schaefer, Bruce Bohne
ACTOR TWO	Allan Hickle-Edwards
ACTOR THREE	Hassan El-Amin, David Lenthall
ACTOR FOUR	David Anthony Brinkley
ACTOR FIVE	James Cada
ACTOR SIX	Emil Herrera, Tim Danz
ACTOR SEVEN	John Seibert
ACTOR EIGHT	David M. Kwiat
ACTOR NINE	Stephen Gee
SINGERS	Leslie Ball, Prudence Johnson, Ruth MacKenzie
MUSICIANS	Eric Peltoniemi, Jeffrey Willkomm, William Mask

Ten November was commissioned by Actors Theatre of St. Paul and was first presented as a staged reading as part of the theatre's First Stage program in the fall of 1986.

PLAYWRIGHT'S NOTE

Standing on the shore you can feel it.

In the summer of 1976 I heard a Gordon Lightfoot song called *The Wreck of the Edmund Fitzgerald*. It was a haunting ballad about what I thought was an ancient maritime disaster. Being a landlocked, lake-stupid Denverite, I thought it was folklore. It was not until years later, after moving to Minnesota, that I discovered it was fact. Recent history. An event still vividly remembered by the people who live on the lakes and bitterly debated by the men who work them.

In the spring of 1986, Actors Theatre of St. Paul's artistic director, Michael Miner, commissioned Eric Peltoniemi and me to create a theatre piece of our choice. After a few months of marginal ideas and exceptional coffee, one day I heard Lightfoot's song again. That afternoon I was standing in line at the library holding 11 books about the Great Lakes and a copy of the Coast Guard report of the sinking. The story had me.

Three things became clear. There would be no attempt to "miniseries" the event; that is, to name, individualize and impersonate the 29 men and their families. Secondly, there would be no attempt to establish blame. Rather, the play would present all the conflicting points of view that surround the *Fitzgerald's* sinking. Finally, the play would be more than the story of a Great Lakes tragedy, it would be Eric's and my response to that story. The focus of this response seemed to be the myth of invincibility in our culture, and our attempts to deal with loss.

We got cocky with nature. Technology has enabled us, we think, to reinvent it in our own image. Our machinery has made us, we think, invincible. Nature is what we do on Sunday. This belief christens our ships, launches our rockets, and bombards our atoms. Ultimately, however, nature refuses to be scenery. In the case of the *Fitzgerald* (and the space shuttle *Challenger* 11 years later), the fallibility of invention was made known to us. Nature is active. It still melts our wings when it needs to. In the case of the *Fitzgerald* sinking, to claim "human error" would be like trying to establish blame for the wind. Nature is both cause and effect. It is the force against which we play out our lives.

Emily Dickinson wrote that "Parting is all we know of heaven, and all we need of hell." Loss is as universal as joy is selective. Our attempts to grapple with loss—through grieving, ritual and reflection—unite us. Loss writes our songs and builds our memorials. It turns the pages of our papers. It challenges our capacity to care. In fact, of late our need for grieving and reflection has not begun to keep pace with the media's ability to discover and report loss. Even the 29 men lost aboard the *Fitzgerald* constitute, by comparison with other disasters, a small tragedy. However, because of their sudden and complete disappearance, the sinking has remained a great mystery. The final moments of the voyage remain, by necessity, fiction. Given no witnesses, there are no factual accounts. With no bodies discovered, there is no grave site, no point of pilgrimage. Even the memorial services which were held annually for 10 years on the anniversary of the sinking have been curtailed. All that remains is the Lake and her stories. The stories are handed down not to resurrect the past, but to inform the present. No one who knows the lakes believes Superior has claimed her last ship.

Eric and I respectfully dedicate this play to the men of the *Edmund Fitzgerald*, to those who have grieved their loss, and to all who are on the lake tonight.

Standing on the shore you can feel it.

CHRONOLOGY
[Compiled by Christine Sumption]

18 September 1679	*The Griffon*, a French ship loaded with furs, was seized in a violent storm on Lake Huron and vanished without a trace.
9 November 1913	The worst storm ever to strike the Great Lakes sank 10 ships and drowned 235 seamen.
11 November 1940	The Armistice Day storm shattered the coal-carrying *William B. Davock* and the *Ann C. Minch* with its load of grain. Fifty-eight crewmen died.
May 1953	The *Henry Steinbrenner* was lost on Lake Superior. Seventeen men were lost.
8 June 1958	The S.S. *Edmund Fitzgerald*—a huge iron-ore freighter—was launched from the Great Lakes Engineering Works. At 729 feet, it was the longest ship ever to be launched on the Great Lakes.
September 1958	The *Fitzgerald* was commissioned for service by the Columbia Transportation division of the Oglebay-Norton Company, a transportation and mining firm with headquarters in Cleveland. "Big Fitz" was the flagship of the company fleet.

17 November 1958	The 640-foot bulk freighter *Daniel J. Morrell* broke in two and quickly sank in a Lake Huron gale, taking 28 of the 29-man crew.
1973	The S.S. *Edmund Fitzgerald's* load-line certificate was changed, effectively permitting the vessel to carry several hundred tons more cargo than had been considered safe when the ship was built.
9 November 1975 2:15 p.m.	At the Burlington Northern Railroad Dock at Superior, Wisconsin, the *Fitzgerald* was loaded with 26,116 long tons of taconite (iron ore) pellets and fueled for the voyage across Lake Superior to Detroit, Michigan.
4:15 p.m.	The *Fitzgerald* caught sight of the *Arthur M. Anderson*, a U.S. Steel ore carrier bound for Gary, Indiana. The two ships proceeded along similar routes.
7:00 p.m.	The National Weather Service issued gale warnings for all of Lake Superior.
10 November 1975 7:00 a.m.	Gale warnings were escalated to storm warnings.

7:15 a.m.	The *Fitzgerald* contacted the company office and indicated a delayed arrival at the Soo locks due to weather conditions.
3:30 p.m.	The captain of the *Fitzgerald* radioed the *Anderson* that he had experienced some topside damage, was taking on water and had a list. He had his pumps going and was slowing down to allow the *Anderson* to catch up.
4:10 p.m.	The *Fitzgerald* radioed the *Anderson* that both radar antennae had been carried away, and that the ship would need navigational assistance.
7:00 p.m.	The *Anderson* had drawn to within nine miles of the *Fitzgerald* and could easily identify the *Fitz* on the radar screen.
7:10 p.m.	A furious snow squall struck. The *Fitzgerald* was no longer visible on the radar screen.
7:15 p.m.	The *Anderson* radioed the *Fitzgerald* to advise the captain that an upbound ship had been spotted ahead of the *Fitzgerald*. In response to an inquiry regarding the earlier troubles, the captain of the *Fitzgerald* remarked, "We are holding our own."

7:25 p.m.	The snow squall ceased. The *Anderson* could no longer see the *Fitzgerald*, either visually or on radar, nor could radio contact be made.
7:39 p.m.	The captain of the *Anderson* called the coast guard station at Sault Ste. Marie to inform the radio operator that he'd lost contact with the *Fitzgerald*.
8:32 p.m.	The captain of the *Anderson* radioed the coast guard again regarding the welfare of the *Fitz*.
8:32 p.m.	The coast guard radioed for assistance from the commercial vessels in the area.
8:40 p.m.	The Coast Guard Great Lakes Rescue and Coordination Center at Cleveland was notified that the *Fitzgerald* was missing. The official search began.
9:00 p.m.	The *Arthur M. Anderson* turned back into the storm to assist in the search for the *Edmund Fitzgerald*.
9:45 p.m.	The coast guard made an urgent broadcast alerting all who could hear that the S.S. *Edmund Fitzgerald* was missing and a search was in progress.
11 November 1975	Various materials from the *Fitzgerald* began to be discovered.

13 November 1975	The active search for the *Fitzgerald* was suspended, although daily and weekly flights were maintained by the coast guard until the end of the year.
18 November 1975	The Marine Board of Investigation convened to look into the loss of the S.S. *Edmund Fitzgerald*.
12 May 1976	The coast guard made a visual survey of the wreckage of the *Fitzgerald* using the U.S. Navy Controlled Underwater Recovery Vehicle, recording videotape, and shooting color photographs.
26 July 1977	The Marine Board of Investigation issued its report on the wreck of the *Edmund Fitzgerald*, concluding that the ship had lost buoyancy due to massive flooding of the cargo hold, and that the sinking was so rapid and unexpected that no one had been able to abandon ship. Safety recommendations were made to prevent similar accidents. It was recommended that "no further action be taken and that this case be closed."

PLAYWRIGHT'S PRODUCTION NOTES

Set: Large, open playing space. Locales designated with light. Various units to serve as tables, chairs, etc. Any literal representation of the boat should be avoided.

Style: Factual. Brutal.

The Songs: They are not transitions from scene to scene. They are entities unto themselves. They tell a story all their own.

The Singers: The three singers' presence should be felt throughout, even in non-musical sequences. They are the environment of the play.

CHARACTERS

Nine Male Actors, various ages.

ACTOR ONE:	Cooper, Lange
ACTOR TWO:	Hilsen, Porter, Coast Guard Three
ACTOR THREE:	Garcia, Speaker, Coast Guard Two
ACTOR FOUR:	Sailor, Murphy
ACTOR FIVE:	Barrow, Unseen Voice
ACTOR SIX:	Young Man, Stenographer
ACTOR SEVEN:	Zabinski, Alien Theorist
ACTOR EIGHT:	Webster, Coast Guard Four
ACTOR NINE:	Larson, Coast Guard One, Man Who Walks Through Scenes

Three Female Singers

Two Musicians

Time: 9 November 1975 to the present.
Place: Lake Superior and its surroundings

ACT I

Ruin is formal, devil's work,
Consecutive and slow—
Fail is an instant no man did,
Slipping is crash's law.
                    Emily Dickinson

Darkness. Silence. Nine pin spots come up on NINE FACES. The FACES are scattered about the stage. THEY speak urgently to the audience.

NINE. Marine Casualty Report. S.S. Edmund Fitzgerald sinking in Lake Superior on 10 November 1975 with loss of life.
    ONE. The search results:
    TWO. Twenty cork life preservers.
    THREE. Eight oars.
    FOUR. One piece of a sounding board. There are no chalk markings on the sounding board.
    FIVE. One large built-up wooden fender block with line.
    SEVEN. Thirteen life rings.
    THREE. One piece of a life ring.
    SEVEN. One wooden stool.
    ONE. Fitzgerald, this is the Anderson. Do you read me?
    EIGHT. Anderson. This is the Fitzgerald.
    ONE. This is the Anderson. Have you picked up the gale warnings the Weather Service just posted? Over.
    EIGHT. This is the Fitzgerald, ah, roger.
    ONE. Fitzgerald, I'm thinking of taking the northern track, get close to the north shore for shelter in case it really starts to blow. Over.

EIGHT. I'm thinking the same. I'm steering sixty-five degrees for Isle Royale.
NINE. One heaving line.
FOUR. One stepladder.
THREE. One rudder from a lifeboat.
SIX. One floodlight.
EIGHT. Anderson, this is the Fitzgerald. I have sustained some topside damage. I have a fence rail laid down, two vents lost or damaged and a list. I am checking down. Will you stay by me until I get to Whitefish?
ONE. This is the Anderson. Charlie on that. Do you have your pumps going?
EIGHT. Yes. Both of them.
TWO. One spray bottle. White. Marked "Pilothouse Window."
NINE. One broken extension ladder.
SEVEN. Pieces of assorted debris.
SIX. Two twenty-five-man inflatable rafts.
FIVE. The entire number two lifeboat, severely damaged.
EIGHT. Anderson, this is the Fitzgerald. I have lost both radars. Could you provide me with radar plots till we make Whitefish Bay?
ONE. Charlie on that, Fitzgerald. We'll keep you advised of your position.
FOUR. The remains of the number one lifeboat. It has been torn in half.
EIGHT. Grand Marais, this is the Fitzgerald. Is the Whitefish radio beacon operative? Over.
THREE. Negative, Fitzgerald. We've had a power failure. Both the Whitefish beacon and the light are inoperative.
TWO. The upright bow section, approximately two hundred seventy-six feet long.
FIVE. The inverted stern section, approximately two hundred fifty-three feet long.

ONE. Fitzgerald, this is the Anderson. Our radar shows you fifteen miles ahead of us and just a shade to the left.
EIGHT. I want to be two to two-and-a-half miles off Whitefish Point.
SEVEN. The debris of the disintegrated midship structure.
SIX. Fitzgerald, this is the Avafors. I have the Whitefish light now, but still am receiving no beacon. Over.
EIGHT. DON'T ALLOW NOBODY ON DECK.
SIX. What's that Fitzgerald? Unclear. Over.
EIGHT. I have a bad list, have lost both radars and am taking heavy seas over the deck.
FOUR. The two sections rest approximately one hundred seventy feet apart—
EIGHT. It's one of the worst seas I've ever been in.
SEVEN. —at a depth of five hundred thirty feet.
ONE. Fitzgerald, this is the Anderson. Have you checked down?
EIGHT. Yes, we have. Over.
ONE. Fitzgerald, we are about ten miles behind you and gaining about a mile and a half an hour on you.
NINE. Despite the intensive search, no survivors were found.
ONE. Fitzgerald, there is a target nineteen miles ahead of us—
NINE. Nor were any bodies recovered.
ONE. —so the target is nine miles on ahead of you.
TWO. Because there were neither witnesses or survivors—
SEVEN. —and because of the complexity of the hull wreckage—
EIGHT. Well, am I going to clear?
THREE. —the actual final sequence of events—
ONE. Yes.
THREE. —culminating in the sinking of the Fitzgerald—

ONE. He is going to pass to the west of you.
SIX. —cannot be determined.
FOUR. Whatever the sequence, however, it is evident that the end was so rapid and catastrophic that there was no time to warn the crew—
FIVE. —to attempt to launch lifeboats or life rafts—
NINE. —to don life jackets—
ONE. By the way, Fitzgerald—
SEVEN. —or even to make a distress call.
ONE. —how are you making out with your problems?
SIX. The twenty-nine crewmen on board are missing and presumed dead.
EIGHT. We are holding our own.
FIVE. It is recommended that no further action be taken and that this case be closed.

(*Song: OLDEN DAYS. The FACES are gone.*)

SINGERS.
OLDEN DAYS, NORTHERN SEA
THERE'S A PICTURE
A THOUSAND GULLS
A HARBOR BAR AND BELL THAT RINGS FOR YOU
    AND ME
OLDEN DAYS, ON YOUR SLEEVE
AND I STILL WEAR
THOSE TATTERED GLOVES
A LIGHT AND LOOK AND LAZINESS THAT
    FOLLOWS ME

WE WERE YOUNG THEN
YOU AND ME
I WAS, THEY WERE, YOU WERE
WAS REALLY NOTHING MORE TO BE
SHINING SILVER
ON THE BAY
I KNOW, I KNOW, I KNOW
I THINK ABOUT IT EVERY DAY

EVERY DAY
I THINK ABOUT IT EVERY DAY

OLDEN DAYS, ON THE RUN
Y'TIP YOUR HAT
REMEMBER THAT
THE ONLY TIME WE OPENED UP WE NEARLY
   WON
OLDEN DAYS, ON YOUR TONGUE
AND RISING LIKE
A YELLOW MOON
ON LABRADORS AND HUNTERS AND A WINTER
   SUN

ALL MY EASTERS
ALL MY SONGS
ALL MY, ALL MY, OH MY
AND EVERYTHING WAS GOING WRONG
SIMPLE-MINDED
LITTLE LOVE
NOW I, I SEE, I KNOW
YOU'VE GOT TO WEAR IT LIKE A GLOVE
JUST LIKE A GLOVE
YOU'VE GOT TO WEAR IT LIKE A GLOVE

(MUSIC *continues under as* LIGHTS *reveal a* YOUNG
MAN (ACTOR SIX). HE *is unwrapping something
wrapped in yellowed newspaper. It is a glass jar with a
cassette tape inside. The jar has been sealed with
candle wax.* HE *speaks to the audience.*)

  YOUNG MAN.
  I have this fascination with loss.
  I have this obsession with disappearance.
  The lake, she is an icy magician.

  I do not know them as individuals.

I have read the books and heard the song and seen the list of names.
But the names do not make the faces appear.
They remain a group.
Working men made fallible by fate.

Each November 10th I go to the memorial service.
I hear the bells chime.
I hear the names read.
I see the flowers and rage thrown on the water.

I was in that storm.
Ten miles behind them.
The lake, she is a curious god.
Disappearances can be deceiving.

(*Return to song. LIGHT on the YOUNG MAN goes out.*)

SINGERS.
OLDEN DAYS, NORTHERN SEA
THERE'S A PICTURE
A THOUSAND GULLS
A HARBOR BAR AND BELL THAT RINGS FOR YOU AND ME
OLDEN DAYS, ON YOUR SLEEVE
AND I STILL WEAR
THOSE TATTERED GLOVES
A LIGHT AND LOOK AND LAZINESS THAT FOLLOWS ME

WE WERE YOUNG THEN
YOU AND ME
I WAS, THEY WERE, YOU WERE
WAS REALLY NOTHING MORE TO BE
SHINING SILVER
ON THE BAY
I KNOW, I KNOW, I KNOW
I THINK ABOUT IT EVERY DAY

EVERY DAY
I THINK ABOUT IT EVERY DAY

(*Song ends. All NINE MEN are gathered onstage. A SPEAKER (ACTOR THREE) speaks from a podium.*)

SPEAKER. On behalf of the Northwestern Mutual Life Insurance Company, proud owners of this new vessel; the Oglebay-Norton Company of Cleveland who have chartered it; and their Columbia Transportation Division who will manage it—I welcome you here to River Rouge, Michigan today. (*Applause.*) The eyes of the Great Lakes are upon us as we christen and launch the largest vessel ever put on these freshwater seas. Seven hundred twenty-nine feet long, with a seventy-five foot beam and a capacity of twenty-six thousand gross tons. (*Applause.*) May God grant this vessel and its men his strength. May the Lake grant this vessel and its men her grace. (*Pause.*) It is now my pleasure to introduce the Chairman of the Board of Northwestern Mutual who will officially christen the boat that will proudly bear his name. Ladies and gentlemen, Mr. Edmund Fitzgerald.

(*ACTOR SEVEN steps forward amidst thunderous applause. HE acknowledges the crowd. He is handed a bottle of champagne by ACTOR FIVE, who then exits. ACTOR SEVEN takes the bottle and aims it at a spot in front of him. Much anticipation. HE swings his arm back, the CHRISTENING PARTY freezes: tableau.
A shaft of LIGHT hits a man standing downstage. This is COOPER (ACTOR ONE). A large, detailed map of Lake Superior, showing the routes of the Arthur M. Anderson and the Edmund Fitzgerald on November 9th and 10th, 1975, appears behind him.*)

COOPER. It's by far the cleanest, the clearest and the coldest of the lakes. So deep that we didn't see its base until fifteen years after we'd walked on the moon. The

Chippewa called it Kitchi Gami. Longfellow dubbed it the Shining Big Sea Water. To the sailors, it's known as the graveyard of ships.

UNSEEN VOICE. (*ACTOR FIVE, offstage, on microphone; amplified, firm, impatient.*) Show us on the map, please.

COOPER. (*Ignoring the Voice.*) When you're on the lake, you don't tell another captain how to do his job. If he confirms that, yeah, he's in danger—you help him out. But you don't get on the radio, the radio's a public thing, you don't get on there and speculate about another man's boat. Some things are unspoken. You got your own business to tend to. You got the weather to wrestle with. And you got your pride.

(*The TABLEAU comes to life: ACTOR SEVEN swings the bottle forward. Cheers and applause. Champagne is poured. The CHRISTENING GROUP moves about, drinking and socializing in half-light. ACTOR EIGHT stands motionless in the center of the group.*)

COOPER. It was bright. Unseasonably warm. The Fitzgerald, with an experienced and and respected captain, first mate and crew, pulled out of Duluth-Superior at 2:15 p.m. on 9 November, headed for Detroit. My ship, the *Arthur M. Anderson,* pulled out of Two Harbors, Minnesota at 3:30 p.m., headed for Gary, Indiana.

UNSEEN VOICE. Show us on the map, please.

COOPER. We got the gale warnings ten minutes later and decided, the captain of the Fitz and me, to take the northern route. (*Indicates the route on the map.*) We'd hug the shore of Isle Royale and head toward the Slate Islands, then turn south past Otter Head and come between Michipicoten and Caribou Islands and into Whitefish Bay. This was pretty common in bad weather, to avoid the dangers of the midsection of the lake. At about 3 a.m. on the 10th, the Fitz—being the faster of the two

boats—overtook us and we followed her at a distance of about seventeen miles. Now, the danger in comin' past Caribou is a shoal that extends north and east of the island. (*Indicates on map.*) It's known as Six Fathom Shoal—six fathoms being thirty-six feet. So, a boat like the Fitzgerald which sat twenty-seven feet in the water had a clearance of only nine feet. And in rough seas, with the boat heavin' and pitchin', that number could easily be cut in half.
UNSEEN VOICE. Continue with the story, please.
COOPER. Coast Guard Chart L.S. 9, which indicates the shoal and which we all used to navigate around the island, had not been updated since *1912*. It was discovered during the Fitzgerald investigation that the shoal extended farther out from the island than any of us knew.
UNSEEN VOICE. Please do not digress. The *story*.
COOPER. At 3:20 p.m. the Fitz went through the Six Fathom Shoal. We received the distress call at 3:35.

(*ACTOR EIGHT speaks from the midst of the christening party. Activity continues around him, as HE stares front.*)

EIGHT. Anderson, I have sustained some topside damage. I have a fence rail laid down, two vents lost or damaged and a list. I am checking down. Will you stay by me till I get to Whitefish?
COOPER. In a storm, speed is all. By slowing down to allow us to catch him, the Fitzgerald ran the risk of being swallowed by the trough of the wave. I asked Captain McSorley if he had his pumps going.
EIGHT. Yes, both of them.
COOPER. These pumps—which can pump a combined total of thirty-two thousand gallons per minute—will empty any water from up *top* which has found its way down into the ballast tanks. But if you've got water coming into the cargo hold down *below*, that's another matter. These aren't battleships. They're just

motorized barges. The bulkheads that divide the cargo hold are not watertight and the cargo hold cannot be pumped. So, although she's built to take a lot of water up on her spar deck, it's said that a pencil hole down in her hull will sink her.

UNSEEN VOICE. Please continue.
COOPER. The men know this about the ship.
UNSEEN VOICE. Captain Cooper—
COOPER. The company knows this about the ship.
UNSEEN VOICE. —please continue.
COOPER. The Coast Guard knows this about the ship. (*Pause.*) The Fitzgerald called again at 4:15.
EIGHT. Anderson, I have lost both radars. Could you provide me with radar plots?
COOPER. It was during this time that the captain of the Avafors, while talking to the Fitzgerald on the radio, claims he heard the Fitzgerald captain shout to someone.
EIGHT. DON'T ALLOW NOBODY ON DECK.
COOPER. At 7:10 we informed him of a vessel nine miles ahead of him.
EIGHT. Well, am I going to clear?
COOPER. We told him the vessel would pass to the west of him. We asked how he was making out with his problems. He responded with his final broadcast.
EIGHT. We are holding our own.

(*The CHRISTENING PARTY disbands, except for ACTOR EIGHT, who stands alone in a shaft of LIGHT. ACTORS TWO, THREE, FOUR and SIX come downstage and stand near COOPER. A huge radar screen lights up. The map disappears.*)

COOPER. At 7:15 in the wheelhouse we looked for him on radar.
THREE. We've lost him.
COOPER. We looked from the window of the wheelhouse.
SIX. I've got the lights of three upbound ships.

TWO. The Nanfri, the Benfri and the Avafors.
SIX. They are approximately seventeen miles ahead.
THREE. I've got nothing ten miles ahead where the Fitzgerald should be.
COOPER. He may have had a power blackout. Look for a silhouette.
TWO. Nothing.
COOPER. We tried the radio.
FOUR. Fitzgerald, this is the Anderson. Over.
COOPER. No reply.
FOUR. Fitzgerald, this is the Anderson. Do you read? Over.
COOPER. Nothing. We thought our radio may not be working.
FOUR. William Clay Ford, this is the Anderson. Over.
COOPER. The Ford, anchored at Whitefish Bay, heard us loud and clear.
FOUR. Have you seen the Fitzgerald pull into the bay?
COOPER. Negative.
FOUR. Have you had radio contact with the Fitzgerald?
COOPER. Negative.
THREE. I've got something on radar.
COOPER. A blip appeared where the Fitz should be.
TWO. Gone now.
THREE. There again.
TWO. Gone.
SIX. You got sea return.
COOPER. Sea return. Waves so high that they are picked up on radar as solid objects.

My men stared at the screen.
Stared at the storm.

In the pilothouse there was silence.

(*ACTORS TWO, THREE, FOUR and SIX disappear. The radar screen fades to black.*)

COOPER. At 7:39 I called the Coast Guard station at Sault Ste. Marie on channel 16—the emergency frequency.
UNSEEN VOICE. Switch to channel 12, Anderson. Leave channel 16 clear.
COOPER. I did this and received no reply on channel 12. Fifteen minutes later I tried again.
UNSEEN VOICE. Soo Control.
COOPER. I told them we had lost the Fitz visually and on radar. They seemed unconcerned.
UNSEEN VOICE. Anderson, there is a sixteen-foot outboard missing in that vicinity. Could you keep an eye out?
COOPER. At 8:32 I called again.
UNSEEN VOICE. Soo Control.
COOPER. SOO CONTROL, THIS IS THE ANDERSON. I AM VERY CONCERNED WITH THE WELFARE OF THE STEAMER EDMUND FITZGERALD. HE WAS RIGHT IN FRONT OF US, EXPERIENCING A LITTLE DIFFICULTY. HE WAS TAKING ON A SMALL AMOUNT OF WATER AND NONE OF THE UPBOUND SHIPS HAVE PASSED HIM. I CAN SEE NO LIGHTS AS BEFORE AND DON'T HAVE HIM ON RADAR. I JUST HOPE HE DIDN'T TAKE A NOSE DIVE.

(*The LIGHT on ACTOR EIGHT goes to black.*)

COOPER. At 9 p.m. we pulled into Whitefish Bay and were asked by the Coast Guard to reverse course, sail back into the storm, and join the other commercial boats in the search for the Fitzgerald. We did so, without hesitation. The only Coast Guard vessel that was operational was three hundred miles, or roughly twenty-four hours away.

As we sailed back into the storm, one of my men spoke his last will and testament into a tape recorder, placed the tape in a glass jar, and sealed it with candle wax.

The search lasted all night. We returned with half a lifeboat. That's all.

By this time, the Fitzgerald had been at the bottom of the lake for twelve hours, having submerged in roughly ten seconds.

(*BARROW (ACTOR FIVE), ZABINSKI (ACTOR SEVEN), MURPHY (ACTOR FOUR) and the STENOGRAPHER (ACTOR SIX) enter from various directions and surround COOPER. The STENOGRAPHER sits, typing.*)

BARROW. (*To Cooper.*) You have stated "He went in close to the island."

STENOGRAPHER. The National Transportation Safety Board investigation. May, 1977. Rear Admiral Winfred W. Barrow.

BARROW. You have stated "I am positive in my own mind he went over that Six Fathom Bank." That is a rather ... *positive* statement. Did you believe that to be true?

COOPER. I still believe that as far as the small-scale chart was concerned. That is what I was using.

BARROW. You believed that to be true at the time you stated it?

COOPER. If that chart says thirty-six feet and the Corps of Engineers are right—or whoever it was that got that—then he went over a thirty-six foot area.

BARROW. You believed *at the time you made this* that he went over a thirty-six fathom bank?

COOPER. Yes, I do.

BARROW. And further on in the transcript it says "I know damn well he was in on that thirty-six fathom spot, and if he was in there—"

COOPER. Six-fathom spot.

BARROW. What?

COOPER. Six-fathom. Not thirty-six fathom.

BARROW. (*Pause.*) Yes. "And if he was in there, he must have taken some hell of a seas." That is an *accurate* description of what you stated at the time?

COOPER. I believe so.

BARROW. And you believed *that* to be true *at the time you stated it?*

COOPER. *Yes, I do.*

BARROW. And the third part of the transcript says "We were concerned that he was in too close, that he was going to hit that shoal off Caribou."

COOPER. The shoal water that extends out from Caribou, yes.

BARROW. In earlier testimony before this investigation, you had concluded that the Fitzgerald was perhaps some four to five *miles* off Caribou. Would you care to comment on what appears to be a contradiction between these two positions here?

COOPER. All we can do is give you what we hauled down as an impression. It was my impression definitely that he was closer than I wanted to be.

(*Long silence.*)

BARROW. And did you communicate this to the Fitzgerald?

(*A MAN (ACTOR NINE) walks through the scene, talking. The OTHERS freeze.*)

MAN WHO WALKS THROUGH SCENES. ... I drowned when I was eight almost eight almost drowned we were with my cousins in Akron not Ohio Akron Colorado and I was swimming in a public pool my cousin's public pool in Akron and there were three of us and my Dad was down in the deep end and it was maybe July or August and we ...

(*The MAN is gone. BARROW and COOPER, not having seen him, are still staring at each other.*)

BARROW. Captain Cooper, *did you communicate this to the Fitzgerald?*

(*Silence. COOPER steps downstage. The OTHER MEN freeze.*)

COOPER. You don't tell a man how to run his ship. You get your iron ore across the lake on time and you keep your mouth shut.

(*LIGHT out on Cooper. LIGHTS up on ACTOR THREE, dressed all in white and holding a golf club. HE stands in the midst of the investigation tableau. HE tees up, takes aim, and swings.*
The swing leads directly into the song HEAVEN BEFORE WE KNOW. The SINGERS sit on three stools as THEY sing. In their midst is a small table with a large pumpkin on it. The pumpkin is uncarved.
During the first chorus of the song, LIGHTS bump up on ACTOR TWO. HE is in short-sleeved work clothes and wears gloves. HE has a large T-wrench and is tightening hatch covers on the spar deck. After this action has been established, LIGHTS bump to silhouette only: tableau. The tableau of the man tightening hatch covers fades to BLACK.
NOTE: This image, like the images in the songs that follow, should be specific, but fleeting. It should not last for more than a few lines of the song. Our focus should pull away from the Singers for a moment to capture the image, then return to them.)

SINGERS.
OLD MOSES WAS IN HEAVEN
BEFORE HE EVER HIT THE CURB

AND THE BOTTLE ROLLED OUT OF HIS HANDS
AND LANDED IN THE DIRT
TWENTY-ODD YEARS LATER
THE BROKEN BOTTLE TURNED TO SAND
AND WASHED DOWN TO THE OCEAN
THROUGH THE HEART OF NO MAN'S LAND

AND SALLY WAS IN PIGTAILS
WHEN THE BOYS LEARNED SHE'D GO DOWN
AND SHE'D DO IT IF YOU SANG A SONG
AND LET HER SING ALONG
NOW SHE'S SLEEPING UP ON THE HILL
WITH EVERY MAN IN TOWN
IF YOU LISTEN BEYOND THE TOMBSTONES
YOU CAN HEAR THE SUN GO DOWN ... SINGIN'

HA HA HA!
WE HOLD OUR SIDES
AND WE LAUGH UNTIL WE DIE
HA HA HA!
HA HA HA ... HEE HEE
HEE HEE HEE ... HO HO HO
HA HA HO HO HO!
COME ON GET READY
WE'LL BE IN HEAVEN BEFORE WE KNOW ... HO
   HO HO!

SO HERE'S TO OLD MAN MOSES
WITH HIS BOTTLE IN THE SEA
AND HERE'S TO LITTLE SALLY
AND THE LOVE SHE GAVE FOR FREE
HERE'S TO EVERYBODY
WHO'S BEEN CRYING FOR SO LONG
AND HERE'S ONE FOR THE SINGERS
WHO'VE BEEN SINGING YOU THIS SONG

HA HA HA!
WE HOLD OUR SIDES

AND WE LAUGH UNTIL WE DIE
HA HA HA !
HA HA HA ... HEE HEE
HEE HEE HEE ... HO HO HO
HA HA HO HO HO!
COME ON GET READY
WE'LL BE IN HEAVEN BEFORE WE KNOW ... HO HO HO!

(*Song ends. LIGHTS reveal a long, narrow table, one end of which faces the audience. The table is set at a rake, with four wooden stools on each side and one stool at the downstage end of the table. There are nine place settings: soup bowls, spoons, coffee mugs. No food or drink are on the table.*
EVERYONE except ACTOR NINE is present. The downstage stool is empty. The OTHER MEN sit on the eight remaining stools, their faces lit by a LIGHT shining up from inside the table.
Following the end of the song, there is a full minute of tactile SOUNDS only: spoons scraping soup bowls, coffee sipped and stirred. The MEN do not look at each other. THEY are busy eating. Finally, as the minute ends ...)

SEVEN. I think if she'd a wanted to kill him, she'd a killed him. She was two feet away. (*Pause.*) It was a publicity thing. (*Pause.*) Why else would she have a name like Squeaky?

(*Several conversations erupt. The table becomes very active. The MEN look at each other, but also continue eating. ACTORS ONE and TWO are singing, trying to remember a rather rowdy sea shanty. The OTHER MEN join in the singing as the scene proceeds.*)

ONE and TWO. (*Singing.*)
FARE THEE WELL O'ER THE WATER ...

THREE. I saw it last week.
ONE and TWO.
FARE THEE WELL ...
FOUR. Saw what?
ONE and TWO.
... O'ER THE SEA ...
SEVEN. Hell kind of name is Squeaky Fromme?
ONE and TWO.
FOR 'TIS ... AH ...
THREE. *Rooster Cogburn.*
ONE and TWO.
'TIS ... AH ...
TWO. Damn.
ONE.
'TIS ... AH ...
TWO. Thought you remembered this.
FOUR. Rooster what?
THREE. Cogburn. It's a movie.
SEVEN. Amazed Ford didn't fall into the bullet.
TWO.
'TIS A *LASS* ...
ONE and TWO.
... THAT BE WAITIN' ...
THREE. John Wayne and—
ONE and TWO.
AND SHE MY ...
THREE. Katharine Hepburn.
ONE and TWO.
... BRIDE WILL BE.
FOUR. Love her.
SEVEN. She's a loony.
FOUR. He shoot anybody?
SEVEN. Shooting an unelected president.
TWO. Second verse.
SEVEN. It's lunacy.
ONE and TWO.
FARE THEE WELL ...
THREE. You really oughta see it.

ONE and TWO.
FARE THEE WELL ... UH .. UH ...
    EIGHT. What time is it?
    FOUR. 7:15.
    FIVE. It's a damn shame.
    TWO.
... ON THE *SWAN'S ROAD* ...
    FIVE. They're at the peak a their damn careers.
    FOUR. Wayne and Hepburn?
    ONE and TWO.
FARE THEE WELL ...
    SIX. Csonka and Kiick.
    ONE and TWO.
... O'ER THE WAVES ...
    SEVEN. She's defendin' herself, you know.
    FIVE. Peak a their careers.
    ONE. That's all I know.
    TWO. C'mon.
    SIX. Shame.
    ONE. That's all I remember.
    TWO. *Try.*
    SEVEN. Anyone defends themself's got a fool for a client.
    SIX. They should never a left the Dolphins.
    FOUR. They fall in love?
    ONE.
FOR THE SEA ...
    THREE. Csonka and Kiick?
    ONE.
... SHE BE ...
    ONE and TWO.
... CALLIN' ...
    FOUR. Wayne and Hepburn.
    EIGHT. That's New York's problem, not ours.
    ONE and TWO.
'TIS A ...
    TWO.
... SAILOR ...

ONE. No.
THREE. Not really. They just argue a lot and ride horses.
FIVE. It's Shula's fault.
TWO.
'TIS A YOUNG MAN ...
FIVE. Shula didn't come up with the money.
ONE. No.
THREE. The gang he's chasin' kills her father.
TWO.
'TIS AN ...
SIX. Shula had nothin' to do with it.
ONE.
... *ORPHAN* ...
TWO. Aha!
EIGHT. Why should Ford bail out New York City?
ONE and TWO.
'TIS AN ORPHAN SHE CRAVES.
SIX. They're just greedy.
FOUR. New York?
SIX. Csonka and Kiick.
ONE and TWO. Third verse.
EIGHT. Ford's got his own problems.
SEVEN. Problems?
FIVE. And you wouldn't a taken that money?
SEVEN. The man's *life* was threatened.
FOUR. That's all?
ONE and TWO.
FARE THEE WELL ...
THREE. No.
ONE and TWO.
... O'ER THE WATER ...
SIX. Not gonna be in their prime forever.
ONE and TWO.
FARE THEE WELL
THREE. They go off chasing this gang that killed her father.

ONE and TWO.
... O'ER THE SEA ...
    FIVE. I mean, christ, anything called the *World Football League.*
    ONE and TWO.
ALL THE MEN ...
    FIVE. They shoulda known better.
    ONE, TWO and SIX.
... WENT BEFORE YOU ...
    EIGHT. New York oughta hire that Dahl guy.
    ONE, TWO and SIX.
THEY BE WAITIN' FOR THEE.
    FOUR. Do they catch 'em?
    THREE. Who?
    EIGHT. Dahl. Jerry or Larry. *Gary.* Gary Dahl.
    FOUR. The gang.
    EIGHT. You know.
    THREE. Of course they do.
    EIGHT. The Pet Rock guy.
    ONE, TWO , THREE and SIX.
FARE THEE WELL...
    EIGHT. Oughta hire him.
    ONE, TWO , THREE and SIX.
... O'ER THE WATER ...
    SEVEN. You remember Manson in the courtroom?
    EIGHT. I think he could save New York.
    ONE, TWO , THREE , FOUR and SIX.
FARE THEE WELL O'ER THE SEA ...
    EIGHT. Any guy that can sell a rock knows his stuff.
    ONE, TWO , THREE , FOUR and SIX.
'TIS A LASS ...
    FIVE. Gonna miss those guys.
    ONE, TWO , THREE , FOUR and SIX.
... THAT BE WAITIN' ...
    FIVE. Warfield, too.
    ONE, TWO , THREE , FOUR, SIX and EIGHT.
AND SHE ...
    SEVEN. She's gonna be worse than Manson.

ONE, TWO , THREE , FOUR , SIX and EIGHT.
...MY BRIDE WILL BE ...
    FIVE. The Dolphins aren't gonna be the same.
    ONE, TWO , THREE , FOUR, SIX and EIGHT.
FARE THEE WELL ON THE SWAN'S ROAD ...
    SEVEN. She said she did it to save the redwoods.
    ALL BUT SEVEN.
FARE THEE WELL O'ER THE WAVES ...
    SEVEN. Yeah. Right.
    ALL BUT SEVEN.
FOR THE SEA SHE BE CALLIN'
'TIS AN ORPHAN SHE CRAVES.
    SEVEN. She was *two feet* away.
    ALL BUT SEVEN.
FARE THEE WELL O'ER THE WATER ...
    ALL.
FARE THEE WELL O'ER THE SEA
ALL THE MEN WENT BEFORE YOU
THEY BE WAITIN' FOR THEE.

(*The MEN laugh, cheer, applaud their song, Some of the MEN exit, some remain at the table.*
Song: WIDOWS OF THE WATER—Prelude. During the second verse of the song. LIGHTS bump up on ACTOR FIVE. HE wears black dress pants and a white T-shirt. HE is shining his black dress shoes with a rag. Once this action has been established, LIGHT bumps to silhouette only: tableau. The tableau of the man shining his shoes fades to BLACK.)

    SINGERS.
ALL OF YOUR JACKIES
ALL YOUR JOLLY YOUNG LADDIES
ALL OF YOUR SUMMER
AND WINTER DADDIES FREE
ALL OF YOUR DARING
AND YOUR DASHING YOUNG SKIPPERS

WIDOWS OF THE WATER
WHERE CAN THEY BE?

ALL OF YOUR SAILING
AND YOUR SALIENT SAILORS
ALL OF YOUR JACKTAR BOYS
AND MARINERS SO FREE
ALL OF THEIR FACES
WITH THEIR BUCKY CHEEKS SO ROSY
WIDOWS OF THE WATER
WHERE CAN THEY BE?

(Song ends. LIGHTS reveal the YOUNG MAN (ACTOR SIX) sitting on the floor speaking into a cassette tape recorder. Near him on the floor is a glass jar, empty.)

YOUNG MAN. The leather jacket to Danny.
The books and records to Sarah.
Toss the "White Album" on the water.
The dog to Dad. Sorry, Dad.
And this letter to be played for my son twenty years from this day and not before.

My dear Joshua. I speak to you in the midst of a great storm on Lake Superior. The Edmund Fitzgerald has been lost. My ship, the Arthur M. Anderson, is now headed back into the storm to search for her. The seas continue to build. We have green water on deck. This will be my last voyage, I'm certain.

As I fight this storm, you lie in a crib in Duluth. Months ago you left the water and entered the world. We are now passing each other.

I have nothing to give you, son, that I haven't already. My guts, my brains, my bald spot. You will have no more of my time, or my face, or my laughter. You will only have my heritage.

I will father you from within.

(*The YOUNG MAN removes the tape from the cassette recorder and is placing it in the glass jar as THE LAKE'S SONG begins. During the song, the LIGHT on the YOUNG MAN fades to BLACK.*)

    SINGERS.
THEY CALL ME LAKE SUPERIOR AND MANY OTHER NAMES
THEY SAY MY GAIN WILL BE YOUR LOSS
THAT I'LL STEAL ANYTHING FROM A LITTLE WEDDING RING
TO SPLINTERS OF THE ONE TRUE HOLY CROSS
TO SPLINTERS OF THE ONE TRUE HOLY CROSS

THEY SAY I'D STEAL THE BABY FROM YOUR ARMS
A THING OF BEAUTY FROM YOUR EYES
BUT ALL I'VE EVER WANTED WAS TO CRASH AROUND AND SING
THESE THINGS THEY TELL ABOUT ME ARE LIES
THESE THINGS THEY TELL ABOUT ME ARE LIES

OUT HERE ON THE WATER THE NIGHT IS DARK AND DEEP
THE STARS ARE LOST UNTO THE SKY
THE WIND IS GETTING STRONG AND THE MOON IS NEARLY GONE
THAT ONCE DID SHINE IN LAKE SUPERIOR'S EYES
THAT ONCE DID SHINE IN LAKE SUPERIOR'S EYES

AGAINST THE BITTER NIGHT A BOW LIGHT GLOWING RED
COLORS ALL THE BLOWING SNOW AROUND
AND WRAPPED UP IN THEIR WEATHERSKINS, THEIR HATS UPON THEIR HEADS
YOU CAN HEAR THE SAILORS SING THIS SONG
YOU CAN HEAR THE SAILORS SING THIS SONG

(*As the song ends, LIGHTS reveal the long narrow table set at a rake, as before. ACTORS ONE, TWO, THREE, FOUR, FIVE and EIGHT sit at the table. The downstage stool is still empty. The MEN eat, as before. SOMEONE reads a paperback. SOMEONE smokes. SOMEONE does a crossword puzzle.*
A shaft of LIGHT on ACTOR THREE. HE turns from the table and notices the audience. HE speaks to them. The OTHER MEN do not look at him.)

THREE.
I am baking a pie.
My pies are legendary.
My pies can launch ships and settle global conflicts.
They disappear like summer and linger like perfume.
My pies.

There is an opera singer in the next room.
An aria from *Aida*.
I am peeking in the oven when I hear the song become a scream.

I slam the oven.
Scream.
I rush to the door.
Scream.
Locked.
Scream.
I reach for my key to the door and it has become a huge brass ring of hundreds and hundreds of keys.
Scream.
I begin to try the keys.
Scream.
One by one by one.
Scream.

At that moment where the mind understands that it will have to try *every single key* on the ring—the fourth key opens the lock.

I am elated.

Scream.

I throw open the door.

I discover another room and across this room another locked door.

Another—

Scream.

The entire room is covered, at a depth of five feet, with keys.

Scream.

I begin to push my way through the keys, grabbing at huge handfuls of them as I go.

I am halfway to the door when the ceiling opens and a barrage of keys falls into the room, burying me.

Holding my breath, I struggle toward the door.

Scream.

With my hand I feel the door.

The scream stops.

(*The MEN stop eating.*)

THREE.

The door opens on its own.

My head emerges from the keys and I view the other room.

It is my kitchen.

I open the oven.
I hear an opera singer.
I remove the pie.
An aria from *Aida*.

I slice the pie.
Scream.

I slice the.
Scream.
I slice.
Scream.
I.

(*Silence, then the MEN resume eating as the LIGHT on them fades.*)

Song: GRAND INLET. During the second verse of the song, LIGHTS bump up on ACTOR EIGHT. HE is in short-sleeved work clothes and wears gloves. HE is mopping the spar deck. After this action has been established, LIGHTS bump to silhouette only: tableau. The tableau of the man mopping fades to BLACK.)

SINGERS.
GRAND INLET
TO THE HEALING ZONE
WHEN I SAW YOU FIRST I WAS IN SHAMBLES
HITCHHIKIN' ALL THE WAY
ON FIFTY CENTS AND A PACK OF CAMELS
I WAS LOOKIN'
FOR EASY MONEY
A WOMAN WITH DYNAMITE AND CHARGES
A WAY TO GET OFF
AND GET IT OFF ON THE SLOW BOAT YEAH
AND JOIN THE BOHEMIANS OUT ON THE BARGES

AND I DID
YES I DID
AND I LANDED
SMACK DAB IN THE HEALING ZONE
AND I DID
YES I DID
AND I LANDED
SMACK DAB IN THE HEALING ZONE

GRAND INLET
TO THE HEALING ZONE
WHEN I SAW YOU LAST I WAS ON CRUTCHES
NOW I'M STANDIN'
OUTSIDE OF YOUR DOOR
LOOKIN' AT IT ALL COME BY IN FLASHES
GRAND INLET
HEALING ZONE
OH HOW THE TIME HAS EASED MY MIND
FROM THAT DAY
WHEN THE DOCK FIRST SLIPPED AWAY
AND WE ROLLED OUT INTO THE MARITIME

AND WE DID
YES WE DID
AND WE LANDED
SMACK DAB IN THE HEALING ZONE
AND WE DID
YES WE DID
AND WE LANDED
SMACK DAB IN THE HEALING ZONE

(*Song ends. LIGHTS reveal the ALIEN THEORIST (ACTOR SEVEN). HE sits in an E-Z- Boy recliner and dips a tea bag repeatedly into his cup of tea. HE wears a cardigan sweater and a bow tie and has reading glasses hung around his neck.*)

ALIEN THEORIST.
I'm not asking you to believe me.
I'm just asking you to listen.

The Coast Guard report mentions an *unidentified object*. Quote.
The topside damage could have been caused by the vessel striking an *unidentified object* in the heavy seas. Both the reduced visibility from the snowstorm and the radar malfunction would, in the opinion of the Marine

Board, have reduced the likelihood that the crew of the vessel could have detected the *object* in sufficient time to take effective action to avoid it.
Unquote.

We really only know two things.
The Edmund Fitzgerald was visible on radar one moment.
The next moment it was gone.

I'm not asking you for money.
I'm just asking you to listen.

29 men.
A 729-foot boat.
A 29-hour journey.
Look at the numbers.
29. 29. 29.
A snychronicity of facts.
Why did we find all the rescue equipment?
Why did the ship's radar give out?
Why did all the other ships on the same lake in the same storm make it safely to port?

Look at the numbers.
2, 9, 2, 9, 2, 9.
Eleven.
The number of the occult.
Eleven what?
Eleventh month.
Gales of November.
Thirty days of autumn and rage.
Look at the facts.

Why never a body found?
Not a bone.
Not a shoelace.

Why, in the recorded history of Lake Superior, has nobody *ever* washed up on its shores?

I'm not asking you to help them.
I'm just asking you to listen.

These men are not missing and they are not dead.

These men were abducted.

There are pockets of the cosmos that we will never understand.
That we must never try to enter.
These pockets are the passageway to the alien world.
Upon entering, your departure is assured.

(*A MAN (ACTOR NINE) walks through the scene, talking.*)

MAN WHO WALKS THROUGH SCENES. ... And the lifeguard had white stuff on his nose and green trunks and I had yellow trunks like my Dad's and my cousins had trunks I don't remember what color and the lifeguard was talking and laughing with his girlfriend who had a red two-piece suit on and long legs and I was ready to jump in ...

(*The ALIEN THEORIST watches the MAN go by. Pause. HE takes a sip of his tea.*)

ALIEN THEORIST.
I believe these pockets in our culture are multiplying.
The aliens love our country.
They lie in wait for us.
They thrive on our Americanism.
They feed on our capitalism.
They depend on our fascination with the disposability of human life.

I'm not asking you to *change*.
I'm just asking you to listen.
Listen *carefully*.
It may have been *them* you heard.

The report mentions an unidentified object.

Be on guard.
A people whose primary aims are driving, shopping and television are subject to terrorism at any time.

Things just don't disappear.
Something takes them.

(*Pause. HE sips his tea. HE stares at the audience. HE snaps his fingers. The LIGHT on him goes out immediately.*
Song: LISTEN ADVERSARY—Prelude. The stage is DARK. The song is sung offstage, on microphone.)

    SINGERS. (*Off.*)
I STICK MY KNIFE THROUGH THE TOP OF THE TIN
I HEAR YOUR BODY RATTLE IN THE WIND
OOOH ...
COMING AFTER ME.

(*Song ends, abruptly. LIGHTS reveal the SAILOR (ACTOR FOUR). HE sits on a wooden crate. In front of him, on a wooden spool, is a ship in a bottle. HE is finishing its construction by pulling on small threads which make the masts and sails rise up and into place inside the bottle. HE continues working on the ship occasionally as HE speaks to the audience.*)

    SAILOR. You should remember that if you'd a stood her up the Fitz would a been the tallest building in the

Midwest. The five hundred thirty feet of water she sank in was not nearly as deep as she was long.

And I don't mean to say she sank.

She was torn in half.

Everybody's got a theory.

The men who work the lakers think she took on water down below from a gash in her hull. The gash, they say, came from shoaling off of Caribou Island. The Coast Guard, some of whom are so damn educated they're stupid, claims she took on water from above through hatch covers that were damaged or not closed tight. Hell, there's even nutheads think she met up with aliens who sank the ship and made off with her crew.

The Lake must get a kick out a these stories.

It's simple, really.

At 7:15 on 10 November, the Fitzgerald got hit by the Three Sisters.

(LIGHTS reveal a metallic table. Sitting at the table are COAST GUARD TWO (ACTOR THREE), COAST GUARD THREE (ACTOR TWO) and COAST GUARD FOUR (ACTOR EIGHT.) On the table is a large model of the Edmund Fitzgerald. The COAST GUARD MEN are applying decals and paint, putting the finishing touches on the model. The primary light source is focused on the model.

Standing between the SAILOR and the Coast Guard table in a shaft of LIGHT is COAST GUARD ONE (ACTOR NINE). He recites from the Marine Casualty Report.)

    COAST GUARD ONE. *(Brisk, business-like.)* Findings of Fact. Item Four. Page 18. Weather.

    COAST GUARD TWO. *(Holding the instructions.)* Apply decal B to Section A.

    COAST GUARD THREE. You got B there?

    COAST GUARD FOUR. This is C. Wait. D.

    COAST GUARD THREE. Where the hell's B?

TEN NOVEMBER 45

COAST GUARD TWO. That it?
COAST GUARD FOUR. That's E.
COAST GUARD THREE. Yeah. We got that.
COAST GUARD ONE. A storm, which was described by a National Weather Service forecaster as, quote, a typical November storm, unquote, was generated over the Oklahoma Panhandle on 8 November and by 0700 on 9 November, this well-defined storm was located over south central Kansas, moving to the northeast.
SAILOR. When you're in a storm, you can look for about every seventh wave to be a big one. Your ship is designed to weather this.
COAST GUARD ONE. The storm intensified rapidly as it passed over east central Iowa, and by 1900 on 9 November, it had an average speed of advance of thirty-seven knots.
COAST GUARD FOUR. Wait. Is this B?
COAST GUARD THREE. Yeah.
COAST GUARD FOUR. Your arm was on it.
COAST GUARD TWO. Apply decal—
COAST GUARD THREE. Yeah, yeah.
COAST GUARD ONE. At this time the National Weather Service issued gale warnings for all of Lake Superior.
SAILOR. But you should remember that these are not lakes. They're the world's eighth sea. Their bottom is littered with the wreckage of six thousand ships.
COAST GUARD FOUR. Do the lifeboats come with this?
COAST GUARD TWO. I don't think so.

(*COAST GUARD FOUR exits to get lifeboats.*)

SAILOR. The men know this.
COAST GUARD THREE. Hand me those.
SAILOR. The company knows this.

COAST GUARD ONE. Page 19. The National Weather Service revised the forecast at 2239 on 9 November—

SAILOR. The Coast Guard knows this.

COAST GUARD ONE. —predicting easterly winds thirty-two to forty-two knots, rain and thunderstorms, waves five to ten feet increasing eight to fifteen feet Monday.

SAILOR. On 9 November '75, the Fitzgerald had been permitted to make one final trip, with the stipulation that it undergo significant repairs before the '76 season.

COAST GUARD ONE. Wave heights refer to the distance from peak to trough and are known as "Significant Wave Height."

SAILOR. It's not that the companies are unconcerned with safety.

COAST GUARD ONE. The actual distance from peak to trough of the highest wave could be as much as *twice* the Significant Wave Height.

SAILOR. But safety doesn't get the bills paid.

(*COAST GUARD FOUR returns with two small life boats for the model.*)

COAST GUARD TWO. (*Referring to a decal.*) This is crooked.

COAST GUARD FOUR. It's fine.

SAILOR. They do manage to put a couple lifeboats on every ship. No sailor thinks the lifeboats'll do him any good. They're not meant to be lifesaving devices. They're known in the trade as "psychological factors."

COAST GUARD THREE. That's all the decals?

COAST GUARD FOUR. Who knows.

SAILOR. Know this. When you sail that lake in that month, you're living on the razor.

COAST GUARD TWO. Wait. Here's more instructions. You know Spanish?

COAST GUARD FOUR. Gimme those.

SAILOR. You're in the wheelhouse. You're sitting eighty feet above the front of the ship. You've lost both radars—which means you have to rely on the radio beacon from Whitefish Point. The Whitefish beacon is not working. You don't have a fathometer—which means to tell how deep a water you're in, one of your men has to go out on the spar deck in the blizzard and drop a hand lead in the water, Mark Twain style.
COAST GUARD ONE. Page 20.
SAILOR. You got wind gusts of sixty miles an hour and you got green water coming over the deck.
COAST GUARD ONE. The storm center passed over Lake Superior—
SAILOR. Not *spray*.
COAST GUARD ONE. —with winds increasing rapidly—
SAILOR. Green water.
COAST GUARD ONE. —thirty-five to fifty knots from the northwest.
COAST GUARD FOUR. Wait. It's not dry there.
SAILOR. You're falling deeper into the water after each wave, the prow of the ship fighting harder each time to regain the surface.
COAST GUARD THREE. That straight?
SAILOR. You've been on the lake twenty-nine hours and now she's grown tired of playing with you.
COAST GUARD TWO. Yeah. It's straight.
COAST GUARD FOUR. Beautiful.

(*During the following, dim shafts of LIGHT discover the SINGERS, one by one, EACH in a different area of the stage, staring at the model.*)

SAILOR. Behind your ship the Three Sisters are building.
The Three Sisters are part of the Lake's mythology. Three huge, consecutive waves.

COAST GUARD ONE. At 1639, the National Weather Service revised the forecast.

SAILOR. They will hit your ship one after another.

COAST GUARD ONE. Predicting northwest winds thirty-eight to fifty-two knots.

SAILOR. The first wave is thirty feet high.

COAST GUARD ONE. With gusts to sixty knots.

SAILOR. It rolls over the deckhouse, across the spar deck toward the front of the ship, and pushes the bow into the water.

COAST GUARD ONE. Waves eight to sixteen feet.

SAILOR. Before you can recover, the second wave hits. It is larger than the first. The angle of inclination into the water increases.

COAST GUARD ONE. At 0700, Fitzgerald reported winds at thirty-five knots.

SAILOR. As the angle into the water increases, the twenty-six thousand tons of taconite pellets in the cargo hold begin to slide forward.

COAST GUARD ONE. Overcast, visibility two to five miles in continuous moderate rain.

SAILOR. As the nose of the ship fights to right itself, the third and largest wave—

COAST GUARD ONE. Temperature 41 degrees.

SAILOR. —the size of a four-story building—

COAST GUARD ONE. Waves ten feet.

SAILOR. —hits the ship.

COAST GUARD FOUR. Seven hundred twenty-nine feet long.

SAILOR. The nose buries itself in the lake and the ship, still under power, submarines to the bottom.

COAST GUARD TWO. With a seventy-five-foot beam.

SAILOR. The taconite pellets rush forward with such force that they sever the ship in two.

COAST GUARD THREE. And a capacity of twenty-six thousand gross tons.

SAILOR. The men are swallowed by the water.

COAST GUARD ONE. The 0700 report was the last weather report received from Fitzgerald.

(*COAST GUARDS TWO, THREE and FOUR exit. Pause.*)

SAILOR. The Three sisters are kind. They take you quickly.
Within ten seconds the ship has settled into the mud, deck lights still shining.
At Duluth-Superior, another freighter is being loaded.
COAST GUARD ONE. By 0100 on 11 November, the effects of the severe storm abated on Lake Superior.

(*COAST GUARD ONE exits. The LIGHT on the model remains. The SAILOR makes a final adjustment to his ship-in-a-bottle.*)

SAILOR.
I crewed the Fitz for seven years.
She was loud in a storm.
Her metal had a scream like no other boat I worked.

The boats I work on now get set on a mantle somewhere and dusted off when they need it.
They are frozen in time.

There've been improvements in the technology since the Fitz was lost.
But technology is not the point.
The point is that when the Lake wants you, she takes you.

She has a technology of her own.

(*The LIGHTS on the SAILOR and on the model of the Fitzgerald fade to BLACK.*

Song: THE CROWS. During the first three verses of the song, LIGHTS rise very slowly on a bare stage. It is a very warm, very sunny afternoon. The MEN arrive onstage, one by one, until ALL NINE are present. ACTOR TWO, carrying a T-wrench, and ACTOR EIGHT, carrying a mop, should arrive first and begin working. Except for EIGHT, ALL THE MEN have large T-wrenches. THEY are tightening imaginary hatch covers on the spar deck of the boat. THEY work in their shirt-sleeves, gloves on their hands. THEY converse silently. SOMEONE takes his shirt off. SOMEONE drinks a Coke. THEY work hard, but the feeling is content, almost serene.)

SINGERS.
IN THE WEE WEE HOURS WHEN UNOPENED ARE THE WEEDS
AND THE DEW IS LYING HEAVIER THAN SLEEP
I'LL DRIVE OFF THE CROWS FROM MY 'WAKENING FIELD
EVERY TIME MY HEART IS DARK AND DEEP

O, WHEN I WAS A ROVER AND WAS GRACEFUL IN MY STEP
SKIPPING LIKE A STONE ACROSS THE SEA
I DIDN'T FEAR NOBODY AND I TRAVERSED ALL THE NIGHT
BORE EVERYTHING WITH CALM AND COURTESY

BUT THEY OF ALL THE BIRDS ARE LIKE A BLACKENED WILL-O-WISP
THEIR EYES ARE LIKE THE SHATTERED BROKEN GLASS
AND THEIR COMING IS OF OLD ... O, THEIR COMING IS FORETOLD
AND THE SONG THEY SING IS "EVERYTHING MUST PASS"

TEN NOVEMBER

(*The stage is now fully lit, MUSIC continues under as the MEN, one by one, take a break from their work and speak to the audience. After EACH ACTOR has spoken his line, HE returns to work.*)

FIVE. Fitzgerald loaded its last cargo at the Burlington Northern Railroad Dock Number 1 East in Superior, Wisconsin on 9 November 1975.

ONE. Fitzgerald completed loading at approximately 1415 and crew members were observed replacing hatch covers.

TWO. Each of the twenty-one hatch covers had to be secured manually using sixty-eight hatch-cover clamps.

EIGHT. The First Cook, 28, reported that his ulcer had not improved. He was replaced for this trip by a Temporary Cook, 62.

FOUR. There were no unusual incidents or occurrences.

THREE. The Cadet, 22, was one trip away from completing the two hundred seventy sailing days required by the Great Lakes Maritime Academy.

SEVEN. This appeared to be a routine loading and departure.

NINE. The Captain, 60, and the First Assistant Engineer, 47, were making their final trips before retirement.

SIX. On the shores of Lake Superior, it was Indian summer.

(*Return to song. The MEN finish their work and gradually leave the stage.*)

SINGERS.
AND SO I WEAR THE SHADOW OF THE DARKNESS LIKE A CLOAK
AND I THROW IT FROM MY SHOULDER TO THE WIND

AND I WATCH IT SAIL AWAY ... O, SO VERY FAR
  FAR AWAY
TILL EVENING AND THE CROWS ARE BACK AGAIN

(*The LIGHTS start to fade as the song is concluding until all that can be seen is the Singer's faces and a small area of LIGHT downstage. In this LIGHT is a tattered life vest. Song ends. LIGHTS go to BLACK.*)

End of ACT I

ACT II

While we were fearing it, it came—
But came with less of fear
Because the fearing it so long
Had made it almost fair.

      Emily Dickinson

Darkness. Silence.

UNSEEN VOICE. (*ACTOR FIVE.*) At approximately 1630 on 10 November, the remote monitoring equipment at Coast Guard Station Sault Ste. Marie indicated that the light and radio beacon at Whitefish Point were inoperative. Several attempts were made to restore the Whitefish Point navigational aids, using the remote controls on the monitoring equipment. These attempts were unsuccessful. A repairman was sent to Whitefish Point.

(*Song: OUT OF THE BLUE. The LIGHT of a flashlight hits the face of ONE OF THE SINGERS. During the song, a REPAIRMAN searches the stage with his flashlight. HE is joined by ANOTHER and ANOTHER until numerous ACTORS are moving about the stage and numerous flashlights are operating. The SINGERS' faces are lit by the flashlights and other flashlights scan the stage. The flashlights are the primary light source.*)

  SINGERS.
BLUE, BLUE, BLUE
YOU KNOW IT FEELS SO RIGHT

WHEN YOU BLOW OUT OF THE BLUE INTO A BLUE,
   BLUE LIGHT

HOLY MOTHER MOLEY
IT'S AN ANXIOUS NIGHT
WHEN YOU'RE PULLING ALL YOUR BLUE OUT OF
   AN UNMANNED LIGHT

BLUE, BLUE, BLUE
YOU KNOW IT FEELS SO RIGHT
WHEN YOU BLOW OUT OF THE BLUE INTO A BLUE,
   BLUE LIGHT

HOLY MOTHER MOLEY
IT'S AN ANXIOUS NIGHT
WHEN YOU'RE PULLING ALL YOUR BLUE OUT OF
   AN UNMANNED LIGHT
NEW BLUE LIGHT

AND I SHIP OUT ON THE LAKERS
AND I SHIP OUT IN THE WIND
AND I LIKE IT WHERE THE WATER SPRAY IS COOL
   UPON MY CHIN
AND I LIKE IT WHERE THERE IS NO LAND
BUT ONLY LAKE AND SKY
AND THE BLUE IS BLUER THAN THE BLUE THAT
   BLEW INTO MY EYE
IN MY EYE

(*All three* SINGERS *start speaking simultaneously.*
   MUSIC *continues under the resulting cacophony.*)

SINGER ONE.	SINGER TWO.	SINGER THREE.
At approximately 1630 on 10 November, the remote monitoring equipment at Coast Guard Station Sault Ste. Marie indicated that the light and radio beacon at Whitefish Point were inoperative.	Anderson, this is the Fitzgerald. I have sustained some topside damage. I have a fence rail laid down, two vents lost or damaged and a list. I am checking down. Will you stay by me until I get to Whitefish?	(*Laughing.*)
HELP ME, HELP ME HELP ME, HELP ME		We were having breakfast and his shirt was on fire!
Several attempts were made to restore the Whitefish Point navigational aids. These attempts were unsuccessful.	Grand Marais, this is the Fitzgerald. Is the Whitefish beacon operative? Over.	(*Laughing.*) It was the funniest thing I've ever seen!
HELP ME, HELP ME HELP ME, HELP ME	DON'T ALLOW NOBODY ON DECK. HELP ME, HELP ME.	HELP ME, HELP ME HELP ME, HELP ME

ALL THREE SINGERS. (*Singing.*)
HELP ME OUT OF THE BLUE
    UNSEEN VOICE. Conclusion Number 13. It is concluded that the outages of Whitefish Point light and radio beacon did *not* contribute to the casualty.

(*Return to song. The REPAIRMEN begin to leave.*)

SINGERS.
BLUE, BLUE , BLUE
YOU KNOW IT FEELS SO RIGHT
WHEN YOU BLOW OUT OF THE BLUE INTO AN
    UNMANNED LIGHT

BLUE, BLUE, BLUE
YOU KNOW IT FEELS SO RIGHT
WHEN YOU BLOW OUT OF THE BLUE INTO AN
    UNMANNED LIGHT

BLUE, BLUE, BLUE
YOU KNOW IT FEELS SO RIGHT
WHEN YOU BLOW OUT OF THE BLUE INTO AN
    UNMANNED LIGHT

(*The last flashlight goes out. The song ends. LIGHTS reveal a long table set at an angle. Glasses of water, notebooks, a gavel. Three chairs are behind the table. The STENOGRAPHER (ACTOR SIX) sits at his machine nearby. A witness chair is at center stage. In another area is a case of beer flanked by several simple wooden stools. HILSEN (ACTOR TWO) stands near the witness chair.*)

    HILSEN. (*Addressing the audience.*) It was clear throughout the investigation that the Coast Guard and the company that owned the Fitz were after the same thing.
    An act of God.
    Something that couldn't be helped.

Something that placed no one at fault.

(BARROW (ACTOR FIVE) and ZABINSKI (ACTOR SEVEN) enter and sit at the table.)

HILSEN. A finding of negligence on the part of the Coast Guard could be embarrassing.

(MURPHY (ACTOR FOUR) enters and sits at the table.)

HILSEN. A finding of negligence on the part of the company could lead to lawsuits by the families of the crew.
This could be catastrophic.

(BARROW pounds the gavel. HILSEN moves to a stool, grabbing a beer.)

STENOGRAPHER. The National Transportation Safety Board investigation.
BARROW. Rear Admiral Barrow.
ZABINSKI. Captain Zabinski.
MURPHY. Thomas Murphy. Oglebay-Norton Company. Attorney at law.

(WEBSTER (ACTOR EIGHT) enters and sits in the witness chair.)

BARROW. Name?
WEBSTER. Captain Delmore Webster.
ZABINSKI. Captain Webster, you were at one time an officer on the Fitzgerald, is that correct?
WEBSTER. That's correct.
ZABINSKI. You served under Captain McSorley on several occasions, did you not?
WEBSTER. That is correct.
ZABINSKI. Captain Webster, would you tell the board how often lifeboat drills were held on the Fitzgerald?

(*HILSEN looks at Webster.*)

WEBSTER. We had boat drills once a week. It was noted in the log.
BARROW. Thank you, Captain Webster. That will be all.

(*WEBSTER joins Hilsen, gets a bottle of beer. LANGE (ACTOR ONE) enters and sits in the witness chair.*)

HILSEN. So, my brother was in Africa.
WEBSTER. I feel a story.
HILSEN. He was in Africa on this safari.
WEBSTER. He's from Bismark.
HILSEN. What's that mean?
WEBSTER. How's he get the idea?
HILSEN. What?
WEBSTER. The *idea?*
HILSEN. He saw a brochure.
BARROW. Name?
LANGE. First Mate Gerald Lange, retired.
HILSEN. So, he's in Africa in this remote little village.
ZABINSKI. Mr. Lange, you were at one time an officer on the Fitzgerald, is that correct?
LANGE. Yes.
HILSEN. This village is right on the equator.
WEBSTER. How do you know it's *right* on the equator?
HILSEN. That's the story.
WEBSTER. Knew I felt a story.
ZABINSKI. You served under Captain McSorley on several occasions, did you not?
LANGE. Yes.
HILSEN. So, there's a man in this village who greets the tourists as they arrive.
WEBSTER. A native.

HILSEN. A native. Black man. Skinny. Yellow teeth. Cobweb lines around the eyes. The tourists ask how near they are to the equator.
WEBSTER. There's not a sign?
HILSEN. No.
ZABINSKI. Mr. Lange, would you tell the board how often lifeboat drills were held on the Fitzgerald?

(*HILSEN and WEBSTER look at Lange.*)

LANGE. We had weekly drills and these drills were so noted in the pilothouse log.
BARROW. Thank you, Mr. Lange. That will be all.

(*LANGE gets a beer, moves to one of the stools, listens to Hilsen. GARCIA (ACTOR THREE) enters and sits in the witness chair.*)

HILSEN. (*Standing at center stage, indicates the following.*) The man answers the tourists by drawing a line in the dirt with his foot. He looks at them. He points to the line.
WEBSTER. The equator.
LANGE. I don't believe it.
HILSEN. Neither did they.
BARROW. Name?
GARCIA. Thomas E. Garcia.
HILSEN. The man points to two wooden posts. One a few yards to his left. One a few yards to his right. (*Moving Stage Left.*) The man walks to the post on his left. The tourists follow.
ZABINSKI. Mr. Garcia, you were at one time a crewman on the Fitzgerald, is that correct?
GARCIA. That's right.
HILSEN. Hanging from the post is a large plastic bucket. In the bottom of the bucket is a small hole—about the size of a pencil.

ZABINSKI. You served under Captain McSorley, did you not?

LANGE. What's the bucket for?

HILSEN. The man pours a jug of water into the bucket. The water drains slowly out the hole in the bottom.

ZABINSKI. Mr. Garcia.

HILSEN. The man crumbles some dried leaves and drops them into the water, so the tourists can see the motion of the water as it drains.

ZABINSKI. Did you hear the question?

GARCIA. Yes.

HILSEN. The water is spinning *clockwise* as it drains.

WEBSTER. Of course it is.

LANGE. Hope they didn't pay for this.

ZABINSKI. Did you serve under Captain McSorley?

GARCIA. Yes.

ZABINSKI. Mr. Garcia, would you tell the board how often lifeboat drills were held on the Fitzgerald?

(*HILSEN, WEBSTER and LANGE look at Garcia.*)

GARCIA. Never.

MURPHY. (*Pause.*) Never?

GARCIA. Yes, sir.

ZABINSKI. None at all?

GARCIA. No, sir.

BARROW. (*Pause.*) Mr. Garcia, let me—

GARCIA. There were none.

BARROW. (*Pause.*) Thank you. That will be all.

(*GARCIA gets a beer and listens to Hilsen. BARROW, ZABINSKI and MURPHY confer. LARSON (ACTOR NINE) enters and sits in the witness chair. HILSEN moves Stage Right.*)

HILSEN. The man walks over—about ten yards—to the post on his right. The tourists follow. On this post is another plastic bucket with a small hole in the bottom. The man pours a jug of water into this bucket. Drops leaves in the water like before.

LANGE. Yeah?

HILSEN. The tourists watch the water.

GARCIA. Yeah, so?

HILSEN. The water in this bucket is spinning *counter-clockwise* as it drains.

WEBSTER. Wait.

GARCIA. How far apart?

HILSEN. Ten yards.

LANGE. It's a trick.

BARROW. Name?

LARSON. John H. Larson.

HILSEN. Listen now. (*Moves back to Center Stage.*) The man walks back to the line he made in the dirt. The line *exactly halfway* between the two posts.

ZABINSKI. Mr. Larson, you were at one time a crewman on the Fitzgerald, is that correct?

LARSON. I was.

HILSEN. He points to the line. The tourists watch.

ZABINSKI. You served under Captain McSorley, did you not?

LARSON. I did.

HILSEN. The man holds the bucket directly over the line. He pours water into the bucket. He drops leaves in the water like before.

ZABINSKI. Mr. Larson, would you tell the board how often lifeboat drills were held on the Fitzgerald?

HILSEN. The water begins to drain. *It does not spin at all.*

ZABINSKI. How often, Mr. Larson?

HILSEN. It goes straight down.

LARSON. I wouldn't say he never had a drill—

HILSEN. It does not hesitate.

LARSON. —but I can't say how often he had one.

LANGE. That's bullshit.

HILSEN. *Straight down.*

GARCIA. Jesus.
WEBSTER. (*Overlapping Garcia.*) Your brother saw this?
HILSEN. Yeah.
LARSON. I would not say it was once a month.

(*HILSEN, WEBSTER, LANGE and GARCIA look at Larson.*)

LARSON. He did not have them that often.
BARROW. Thank you—
LARSON. He did *not* have them regularly.
BARROW. That will be all.
HILSEN. The man with the cobweb eyes pointed to the line in the dirt, then turned and walked away. (*HE turns and starts to leave.*)
BARROW. Mr. Hilsen.

(*HILSEN stops.*)

BARROW. Be seated.

(*HILSEN takes the witness chair. LARSON moves and gets a bottle of beer. WEBSTER, LANGE, GARCIA and LARSON watch the investigation from their positions around the stage. ZABINSKI approaches Hilsen.*)

ZABINSKI. Mr. Hilsen, you indicated that the lifeboat station was the Number 1 Boat. Was that on the port or starboard side?
HILSEN. There again, I can't be specific. I always get that mixed up.
ZABINSKI. Mr. Hilsen, who are you kidding? Any boat you were ever on—how many ships did you say you were on?
HILSEN. About twenty-five.

ZABINSKI. Every ship you were ever on, Boat 1 was on one side and Boat 2 was on the other side and don't try to kid me.

HILSEN. I am not.

ZABINSKI. Don't tell me you were on twenty-five ships and you don't know where the Number 1 Boat is. This is a very serious matter here, and you have been evasive on every answer you have given, and I am fed up. Now, you answer. *What side is the Number 1 Boat on?*

HILSEN. Port side.

ZABINSKI. Are you sure of that?

HILSEN. No, sir. I am not.

ZABINSKI. You're damn right you are not. You are not sure about anything. I don't know where you got your lifeboat certificate, but I will be darned if I don't check up on it. (*Very agitated.*) Who are you kidding? What boats were you on? You say you have been sailing since '64. What boats have you been on since '64?

HILSEN. Well, we will go back to the Fitzgerald, and before that was the Mathiott, and I have been on the Armco. I have been on a number of them.

ZABINSKI. Mr. Hilsen, I am not going to dignify you by asking you another question.

(*ZABINSKI looks to BARROW, who stands immediately and approaches Hilsen. ZABINSKI returns to his seat.*)

BARROW. As closely as I can tell, when you first started testifying, you said that you can't recall any boat drills being held on the Fitzgerald, is that correct?

HILSEN. That is correct.

BARROW. I have testimony here taken just yesterday from two people. In that testimony it was stated by one person, "We had boat drills once a week. It was noted in the log," in describing the boat drill.

(*LANGE finishes his beer and leaves.*)

BARROW. Another witness: "We had weekly drills, and these drills were so noted in the pilothouse log." Both stated that in testimony under oath. *You* testified here that you had *no* boat drills on the Fitzgerald.
HILSEN. None that I can recall.
BARROW. You persist in that?
HILSEN. Yes, sir.

(*BARROW turns to Murphy, exasperated. MURPHY stands and addresses Barrow and Zabinski.*)

MURPHY. I am just as concerned about this as you are. I want to say for the record that the entire testimony as it has come in today is just as much a surprise to the company as it is to the board. We are just as concerned at getting to the bottom of it as the board is.

(*WEBSTER finishes his beer and leaves. MURPHY approaches Hilsen.*)

MURPHY. Mr. Hilsen, do you say on oath that you never had a boat drill during the period you were aboard the Fitzgerald with Captain McSorley? Are you telling these people that?
HILSEN. As I said before, I can't recall. I can't say that there never was one held, but as far as I can recall there were none.
MURPHY. But you are saying, then, that they were not held on a *regular basis*. Is that what you are saying?
HILSEN. Yes, that is true.
MURPHY. And you are *saying that under oath?*
HILSEN. I am saying that.

(*LARSON finishes his beer and leaves.*)

BARROW. Do you have anything further to add to your testimony?

HILSEN. Well, I apologize for any shortcoming I may have shown here. I have tried to be helpful.
BARROW. I think the *point*, Mr. Hilsen, is that you have qualified everything you have said before this board by "you can't remember" or "you can't recall." Just about everything you have said.
HILSEN. I am—

(*BARROW pounds the gavel, cutting off Hilsen. BARROW, ZABINSKI, MURPHY and the STENOGRAPHER are gone.*
Song: RIVER IN THE SEA. *The introductory lines of the song alternate with GARCIA speaking to the audience.*)

GARCIA. So, the former officers said drills were held. And the former crewman said they were not.
SINGERS. (*Singing.*)
WATER AS BLUE AND GRAY AS STEEL ... KAREE!
GARCIA. When the Casualty Report was released, it read: "Lifeboat drills were held on the Fitzgerald during the 1975 season, but were not held on a *regular basis* as required by regulations."
SINGERS.
ECHOING LIKE A HORN ... KAREE!
GARCIA. "The present requirement for posting a *placard* containing life-raft launching instructions is not considered sufficient to train crew members in the proper use of this primary lifesaving equipment."
SINGERS.
HEAR THE CRY
OF THE HAWKS THAT FLY
WHERE THE THUNDERHEADS ARE BORN ...
KAREE!
HILSEN. (*Softly, to himself.*) It went straight down.
SINGERS.
FEW ARE REMEMBERED

GARCIA. When asked about the use of lifeboats and life rafts, a former captain said:
SINGERS.
FEW ARE REMEMBERED
GARCIA. "If I was goin' down, I'd crawl in my bunk and pull the covers over my head."
SINGERS.
FEW ARE REMEMBERED ... KAREE!

(*LIGHTS go to black on HILSEN and GARCIA. During the second verse of the song, LIGHTS bump up on ACTORS TWO, FOUR and SIX. THEY are sitting on three stools and in their midst, on a small table, is a pumpkin. THEY are carving it. EACH OF THEM has a mug of coffee. After this action has been established, LIGHTS bump to silhouette only: tableau. The tableau of the men carving the pumpkin fades to BLACK.*)

SINGERS.
SLEEPING ON AND ON IN THE GARDEN OF THE WATER
DREAMING OF THE ORIGINS OF IRON
DRIZZLE OF THE RAIN UP THERE ON THE SURFACE
WASHING EVERY MOLECULE OF TIME

RIVER
RIVER TURN
RIVER THAT FLOWS OUT THROUGH THE SEA
RIVER
RIVER TURN
TAKE TIME FOR A STRANGER LIKE ME

LYING ON MY BACK I SEE THOSE LITTLE WINDOWS
THE SILVER CLOUDS OF FISHES DO EXPOSE
AND FAR AWAY THE GULLS, I HEAR THEM FALL AND SCREAM

ABOVE THE LAKEHEAD WHERE THE TIMBER
  GROWS

RIVER
RIVER TURN
LAY DOWN YOURSELF IN ECSTASY
RIVER
RIVER TURN
RIVER THAT FLOWS OUT THROUGH THE SEA
TAKE TIME FOR A STRANGER LIKE ME
KAREE!

(*Song ends. LIGHTS reveal the long, narrow table set at a rake with nine stools, as in Act I. ACTORS FOUR, FIVE, SIX, SEVEN and EIGHT sit at the table. The downstage stool is empty, as before. ACTORS FOUR, SIX, SEVEN and EIGHT play cards.*
A shaft of LIGHT on ACTOR FIVE. HE turns from the table and notices the audience. HE speaks to them. The OTHER MEN do not look at him.)

FIVE. I have all these strings attached to my fingers.

When I was a child of six, obese from the constant consumption of Big Hunk candy bars, a mystery began to develop. There in the safety of our split-level suburban home, a force was at work.
 A force both deadly and invisible.
 The evidence was irrefutable.
 Our TV trays were missing.
 The TV trays—four of them—that always leaned against the inside right wall of the coat closet, immediately behind my father's beige trench coat with the imitation rabbit-fur collar that he had never worn. The TV trays that, when wiped down with a warm rag, became Thanksgiving tables for me, my sister, my Uncle Dave the chimney sweep, and my cousins Edward and Thomas. The TV trays that, when strategically

placed and covered with a large blanket, became a fort inside which pacts were made that affected our lives greatly until the rain stopped. The TV trays that were always, always there.

It was a Tuesday evening when my mother asked me to get out the TV trays so we could all eat our soup in the family room and watch Red Skelton.

I turned the knob.

The closet has not been disturbed.

The jigsaw puzzles and winter scarfs on the single shelf.

The coats like hopes hung from the metal bar.

My secret stash of Big Hunk bars in the vest pocket of my father's trench coat.

I reached behind the coat for the familiar cool metal feel of the white trays with their "waves of grain" pattern.

Missing.

Gone.

My father turned off Red Skelton for the first time I could remember. The house, yard and garage were searched. Neighbors and friends were called. We had not lent them out. We had not sold them at our garage sale. My sister remembered seeing them in the closet only the day before, which was of little help other than explaining the occasional disappearance of my Big Hunk bars.

My father sat us on the floor, looked in our eyes and said the only words of his that I have never forgotten:

Things just don't disappear.
Something takes them.

To this day I tie a string around everything I value.
I have all these strings attached to my fingers.

(*LIGHTS out on the table. Song: THE CAPTAIN AND THE CADET. Roughly halfway through the song, LIGHTS rise slowly, revealing a sunny afternoon on the spar deck. The table and stools are still in place. The PORTER (ACTOR TWO) drapes a white linen tablecloth over the table. HE also brings on chilled champagne, a tray of glasses and a box of cigars. ACTORS THREE and FIVE appear. THEY begin to play shuffleboard in one area of the stage. THEY wear white, upper-class leisure garb.)*

SINGERS.
THERE ONCE WAS A CAPTAIN AND A LITTLE CADET
A LITTLE CADET WITH A SMILE (YOU BET!)
AND HE HUFFED AND HE PUFFED ON HIS CIGARETTE
AND TRIED TO LOOK SO BRAVE

HE MUSTERED UP A SIDELONG GLANCE
MUTTERED TO THE CAPTAIN, "DO WE HAVE A CHANCE?"
WHILE ALL AROUND THE WAVES DID DANCE
LIKE THE WALLS OF A TOWERING GRAVE

THE CAPTAIN SAID WITH A WISTFUL SMILE
(A LITTLE BIT WISTFUL, BUT IT STILL WAS A SMILE)
"JUST HANG ON, IN A LITTLE WHILE
THE WHOLE DARN THING'S GONNA ALL BE OVER."

UP IN THE HIMALAYAN WIND
THEY SAY YOU CAN SEE THOSE PRAYER WHEELS SPIN
AND THEY ALL GO ROUND AND ROUND AGAIN
LIKE AN ENDLESS S.O.S.
AND I KNOW IT'S JUST A FANTASY
BUT MAYBE THROUGH SOME MYSTERY
A MONK ONCE PUT ONE OUT FOR ME
EMBLAZONED WITH MY NAME

AND THERE IT STILL SITS ALL ALONE
UP SOME LITTLE CAIRN OF STONES
WOULD SOMEONE PLEASE PICK UP THE PHONE
THAT'S ON THE OTHER END?

THERE ONCE WAS A CAPTAIN AND A LITTLE CADET
A LITTLE CADET WITH A SMILE (YOU BET!)
AND HE HUFFED AND HE PUFFED ON HIS CIGARETTE
AND TRIED TO LOOK SO BRAVE.

THERE ONCE WAS A CAPTAIN AND A LITTLE CADET
A LITTLE CADET WITH A SMILE (YOU BET!)
AND HE HUFFED AND HE PUFFED ON HIS CIGARETTE
AND TRIED TO LOOK SO BRAVE

(*Song ends. The PORTER, holding champagne, addresses the audience.*)

    PORTER. It is common practice for the ore carriers to have guest quarters. Elegant dining rooms with expensive china. Plush bedrooms with marble fireplaces. Chandeliered lounges complete with wet bar.
    THREE. Porter.

(*PORTER moves and pours champagne for THREE and FIVE as THEY play shuffleboard.*)

    PORTER. To the officials of the company which owns the boat, and to their families and friends, the trip across Superior is a vacation. A cruise. The long spar deck is perfectly suited for lounging, tanning, shuffleboard, and make a wonderful driving range.

(*THREE and FIVE talk to each other, and to the audience, as THEY continue their game.*)

THREE. 9 November 1913.
FIVE. The storm which has come to be known as the most destructive ever on the lakes.
THREE. On Superior, two ships and fifty-seven men lost.
FIVE. The Hamonic and the Cornell.
THREE. On Huron, *every one* of the eighteen ships on the lake was wrecked.
FIVE. The Wexford, the Hydrus, the Regina, the Argus—
THREE. (*Overlapping.*) Eight were lost completely, as were their hundred and seventy-eight crewmen. The total was twenty ships driven ashore—
FIVE. (*Overlapping.*) —the John A. McGean, the Isaac M. Scott, the Charles S. Price—
THREE. (*Overlapping.*) —ten ships sunk—
FIVE. —the James C. Carruthers.
THREE. —two hundred and thirty-five lives lost.
FIVE. As the bodies began to drift ashore—many frozen together in clusters of ice—they were collected, put on wagons and driven to furniture stores which had been converted to funeral homes.
THREE. Oddly enough, many bodies washed up wearing life preservers from ships they *had not been on.*

(*ACTOR ONE enters, dressed in white garb and carrying a golf club. HE moves downstage to a small piece of turf.*)

FIVE. A young sailor had transferred from the sunken James C. Carruthers without notifying his family. He arrived in his home town as his own funeral was in progress.

THREE. Of the two hundred or so corpses, four were left unclaimed. They were buried with a single tombstone.
FIVE. The tombstone was engraved with one word:
THREE. "Sailors."
ONE. FORE! (*HE swings and drives a golf ball into the lake.*)

(*A few lines of the song QUI A TEMPS A VIE (Song of the Griffon) are heard. ACTOR SIX enters, also in white and also with a golf club. HE joins ACTOR ONE.*)

SIX. Porter.

(*PORTER pours champagne for One and Six.*)

ONE. 16 September 1679.
SIX. At a shipyard near Niagara, established by the Franciscan friar Louis Hennepin, a sixty-foot boat—
ONE. The Griffon.
SIX. —was christened and launched.
FIVE. Its captain was the French explorer René Robert Caveler, Sieur de La Salle.
ONE. Its cargo was trinkets which were to be traded for furs.
SIX. When first put onto the water, La Salle is reported to have said:
THREE. HIGH ABOVE THE BLACK CROWS SHALL THE GALLANT GRIFFON SOAR.
ONE. To the amazement of the Iroquois Indians, who had chosen never to tempt the dangerous midsection of the lake, the Griffon sailed away.
FIVE. Its trip across Erie was serene.
SIX. However, it encountered a storm on Huron. Its crew, having never seen a storm of such magnitude, fell to their knees and prayed.
ONE. Monsieur Lucas, the Griffon's pilot and a former ocean navigator, screamed at La Salle:

THREE. YOU HAVE BROUGHT ME TO MEET MY DEATH ON A NASTY LAKE, INSTEAD OF HONORABLY ON THE OCEAN.
SIX. Suddenly, the storm ceased.
ONE. The Griffon arrived safely in Green Bay, loaded a fortune in furs, and prepared for the trip back to Niagara.
SIX. La Salle, having conquered the Great Lakes, said goodbye to his men and remained behind to search for the headwaters of the Mississippi.
FIVE. The Griffon sailed back across Huron—
ONE. —thereby being the first attempt to transport cargo across the Great Lakes.

(*ONE, THREE, FIVE and SIX lift their glasses in a toast. The PORTER finishes the story.*)

PORTER. Named after a mythical creature with the body of a lion and the head and wings of an eagle, the Griffon disappeared on Huron without a trace.

(*A MAN (ACTOR NINE) walks through the scene, talking. The OTHERS freeze.*)

MAN WHO WALKS THROUGH SCENES. ... And when I jumped I thought I was in the four foot but I wasn't I was in the deep end and my head filled up with chlorine and my feet looked so white and my body hit the bottom where a black line was painted and everything seemed to curve and my Dad pulled me out and laid me on a towel and walked up to the lifeguard who was still talking to his girlfriend and punched him in the face as I lay there choking up water with my Dad holding my head and people staring down ...

(*The MAN is gone. Another few lines of the song QUI A TEMPS A VIE. ONE, THREE, FIVE and SIX sit at the table, sipping champagne and smoking cigars.*

ACTOR EIGHT enters in a white robe, carrying a magazine.)

EIGHT. Porter.

(The PORTER sets up a lawn chair for ACTOR EIGHT and pours him some champagne. EIGHT settles into the chair and speaks to the audience.)

EIGHT. 26 November 1966. The six hundred sixty-foot Daniel J. Morrell was sixty years old. It was built of steel that had not been used since 1948 because it was discovered to be highly brittle at temperatures below the freezing point. As the Morrell was completing its final scheduled trip of the season, they were contacted by the Cleveland headquarters of the Bethlehem Steel Corporation.

SIX. We have failed to meet our yearly tonnage requirements. An additional trip is necessary. We regret this change in plans.

EIGHT. This meant another trip across Huron and Superior to Taconite Harbor, Minnesota.

SIX. FORE! *(HE drives a golf ball into the lake.)*

(SIX joins the other men. THEY listen to the story. LIGHTS slowly focus down to ACTOR EIGHT in his chair.)

EIGHT. With winds on Huron at sixty-five knots and waves at twenty-five feet—the sixty-year-old Daniel J. Morrell began to *break in half*. Its steel plates began to scream as they gave way to the water.

The Deck Watchman, 26, stood on the deck of the rear portion of the boat with twelve other men. Having been awakened by emergency alarm in the middle of the night, none of the men were fully clothed. They were congregated around a single lifeboat. They had decided not to try to throw the boat overboard and jump into it.

Instead, they would ride the sinking ship down into the lake until the lifeboat met the waterline.

Standing there in the freezing rain, the men watched as the front half of the boat completely severed itself from the rear—but *did not sink*. It floated lifelessly as the rear section, still under power, forged ahead—pushing the front section out of its way. The men watched the front half of the boat completely *reverse direction* in the high seas and *sail back past them* into the night, lights still blazing.

The men waited now for the gaping hole left in the center of the boat to fill with water and take them down. Instead, a thirty-foot wave washed the men and the lifeboat overboard in an instant. Of the thirteen, four men—including the Deck Watchman—found their way to the surface and into the lifeboat.

(*HE opens his robe, revealing a white swimsuit underneath. HE applies suntan lotion to his body as HE speaks.*)

They floated all night in the frigid water.

They fired flares which were never seen.

The Deck Watchman rummaged through the lifeboat for a can of oil he intended to smear on his naked legs to protect them from the cold. One of the other men, thinking it was unimportant, had thrown the oil overboard.

The lifeboat fought the waves all night.

Two men died before dawn.

A third died the following afternoon.

As the boat continued to drift, the Deck Watchman piled their corpses on himself for warmth.

At four in the afternoon, after fifteen hours in the water, a Coast Guard helicopter spotted three frozen bodies drifting in a lifeboat.

As the bodes were untangled, the Deck Watchman was discovered beneath them.

Frostbitten and in shock, he reached an arm into the air for help.

(*LIGHTS return to the full stage.*)

    FIVE. He's twenty-six and he didn't panic.
    PORTER. Not until the Morrell was a full *thirty-six hours* overdue did the Bethlehem Steel Company contact the Coast Guard.
    SIX. (*Returning to the piece of turf.*) Soo Control, our ship, the Daniel J. Morrell, is a bit late arriving at the Soo locks. We have yet to meet our tonnage requirements. Could you make some calls?
    PORTER. The sailors work the boats well into November.
    SIX. FORE! (*HE hits a golf ball into the lake.*)
    PORTER. The rich ride them in July.

(*SONG: QUI A TEMPS A VIE. LIGHTS fade as the MEN exit—laughing, smoking and drinking champagne.*)

    SINGERS.
ASSIS AU PONT DU BATEAU
PENDANT QUE LE MUR DES FLOTS
S'ÉLEVAIT AUTOUR
SI HAUT, SI HAUT, SI HAUT, SI HAUT
LE CAPITAINE DISAIT CES MOTS:
"QUI A TEMPS A VIE

"SUR LE LAC SUPÉRIEUR
RASSUREZ-VOUS NAVIGATEUR
SUR LE FROID LAC DES LARMES
HÈ, SOYEZ SANS CRAINTE, MON CADET
MON CADET
QUI A TEMPS A VIE"

"JE VEUX VIVRE MON CAPITAINE"

"CHUT CADET ... CHUT CADET"

"JE VEUX VIVRE MON CAPITAINE"

"CHUT CADET ... CHUT CADET"

"O, JE VEUX VIVRE MON CAPITAINE"

"CHUT CADET ... CHUT CADET ... CHUT CADET"

(*Song ends. LIGHTS reveal the long, narrow table set at a rake, as before. The stool at the downstage end of the table is empty. ACTORS THREE, FOUR and SEVEN are present. ACTORS THREE and FOUR are playing backgammon at the upstage end of the table. ACTOR SEVEN sits on one of the downstage stools.*
A shaft of LIGHT on ACTOR SEVEN. HE turns from the table and notices the audience. HE speaks to them. The OTHER MEN do not look at him.)

SEVEN.
I am watching my good friend be chased by a beast.
He moves through rooms and down streets, frantically in search of safety.
I follow him everywhere, my eyes very near his face, my vision reckless like a hand-held camera documenting his trauma.
He runs and screams and is unable to lose the beast that chases him.
His terror is palpable.

I never see the beast, but sense him ever near.
I am not in danger.
I am moving alongside my good friend, a neighbor to misery, but I feel safe.
Voyeuristic.
Cocky.

My eyes widen as the chase continues.
My friend is exhausted. Barely able to move.
I watch his agony like TV.
I see him cornered.
I sense the beast closing in on him.
My eyes widen into moons.
I strain to see the beast as he approaches, camouflaged in shadow.
At the moment when I sense my good friend's murder by the beast—I realize what the beast is.

(*The MEN pause in their game.*)

SEVEN. He is me.

(*The MEN resume their game.*)

SEVEN. I approach my good friend and now a crowd is cheering.

When in Spain, they say.
When in Spain.

My friend flashes the red cape and I charge.
I graze the cape with my horns as he shimmies aside.
The crowd is ours.
I begin to understand.
I am not a beast and he is not a victim.
We are accomplices.
We are an amusement.
We control the public emotion.
We seduce them with our frantic grace.

When in Spain, they say.
When in Spain.

I paw the earth. He adopts the pose.
Rush and release.

Again and again.
I love the sound and the spectacle.
I cock my head and charge again—as the spear enters my flesh.
My friend accepts the cheers.
We are accomplices.
A second spear near the first.
We are an amusement.

A color I've never seen, a color my body has housed in secret, leaves me and litters the ground.
The crowd is aroused.
My good friend's smile is dry and his stare is wet.
I begin to understand.
He drives the dagger into the top of my head.
I feel it sever my brain.
I feel it pierce the thought of itself.
Rush and release.
Again and again.
In a grotesque slow motion, the crowd erupts.
Children are tossed in the air.
My good friend steps back and wipes his mouth with a sleeve.
I stumble into the burgundy mud.

(*The MEN pause in their game.*)

SEVEN. Tentatively at first, then with abandon, the liquid leaves me.

When in Spain, they say.
When in Spain.

(*The LIGHT on the table fades to black. Song: LISTEN ADVERSARY. During the second verse of the song, LIGHTS bump up on ACTOR FIVE in the same place where we saw him shining his shoes in Act. I. He wears black dress pants, black shoes, white shirt, HE is tying a black tie around his neck. After this action has been established, LIGHTS bump to silhouette only: tableau. The tableau of the man tying his tie fades to BLACK.)*

SINGERS.
LISTEN, ADVERSARY
COMING AFTER ME
LISTEN, ADVERSARY
COMING AFTER ME
I STICK MY KNIFE THROUGH THE TOP Of THE TIN
I HEAR YOUR BODY RATTLE IN THE WIND
OOH ... COMING AFTER ME

I CAN HEAR THE RUMBLE IN THE WESTERN SKY
SOUNDS LIKE A BUNCH OF ROCKS
COMING DOWN ON A DRUM
I HIT A SPARROW IN THE UNDERPASS
AND LEAVE IT ROLLING IN THE BUSTED GLASS
OOH ... COMING AFTER ME

LOOK AT THE TRAFFIC
WON'T YOU LOOK AT THE TRAFFIC
STARTING TO FLOW, STARTING TO FLOW
COMING AFTER ME
AND LOOK AT THE PAPER
THE PIECES OF PAPER COME OUT OF THE ALLEY
THEY'RE SWIRLING AROUND, SWIRLING AROUND
COMING AFTER ME

THE CRIES OF CHILDREN MINGLE
WITH THE BARKING OF THE DOGS
DOWN BELOW THE FACTORY
THE WATER'S LAPPING AT THE LOGS
LISTEN, ADVERSARY
LISTEN, ADVERSARY
LISTEN, ADVERSARY
COMING AFTER ME

(*Song ends. LIGHTS reveal ACTORS TWO, FOUR and SIX sitting on three stools as before. The pumpkin, now completely carved, sits on the small table in their midst. Three coffee mugs are on the table as well. ACTOR FOUR lights the candle inside the pumpkin. The MEN rise and stand immediately behind the stools, as the SINGERS move to the stools and sit. During the following scene, the SINGERS sip coffee, look at the pumpkin, etc. When EACH SINGER'S story is told by the man standing behind her, SHE stops what SHE is doing and simply stares forward. EACH MAN looks at the woman he is speaking of and at the audience, but not at the other two men or women.*)

TWO. I was hanging a picture in the living room when the phone rang. My sister had seen a news flash on TV. A ship was missing on Superior. She said it was my husband's ship.

FOUR. Years ago, when we were first married, he was shingling the roof and he fell. I'm fine, he said. It's a bump. I hated him when he was stubborn and he was stubborn a lot. He couldn't abide being cared for. I'm fine, it's a bump. Let me lay down.

Somehow I drug him to the hospital. All the way in the car I had to listen to his tough stories about falling from this and being hit by that and hell, this is just a *bump*.

It was a concussion.

They told me to give him some pills.

And they told me to keep him awake.

No sleep, they said. Right, I said.

Teach a mule to tap dance.

No problem.

TWO. I called the TV station and they confirmed the report.

The local radio station confirmed it, too.

They said they'd announce any further developments.

I looked at the nail I'd driven into the wall.

A missing ship was not uncommon.
Often, in bad weather, a ship would alter its course and wait out a storm near Isle Royale or some other protected spot. Or there'd be a radar malfunction, a radio gone haywire, and the ship's position would be unknown for a few hours. Eventually, the ship would contact the Coast Guard, reestablish its course, and the announcement would be withdrawn.
I stood listening to my radio.
There hadn't been a loss on Superior in twenty-two years.
I guess we get complacent.
Or worse.
Brave.

(*MUSIC begins, softly.*)

I looked at the nail I'd driven.
I picked up the picture.
I hung the picture on the nail.
I stepped back from the wall.
A Bob Dylan song.
The picture is not straight.
I step forward.
Straighten it.
Step back.
It's not straight.
I step forward.
Straighten it.
Step back.
No further developments.
I stare at the picture.
I don't remember now what it was even a picture *of*.
I just remember that it was never straight.
An hour went by.

I kept tilting it slightly to the left, slightly to the right, stepping back, stepping forward.
Another hour.
Another goddamn Dylan song.
My cheeks are wet.
No further developments.
I'm singing with the radio now.
I'm inventing words.
I'm driving nails into the wall.
Sobbing and singing.
Straightening this goddamn picture.

The station goes off the air.
The TV is snow.
I turn off the light.
I sit on the floor.
In the darkness, I stare at the picture on the wall.

(*Song: THE STRANGER. This verse is sung by the SINGER in front of Actor Two.*)

    SINGER ONE.
WOULD YOU LOOK AT ME.
LIKE I WAS A STRANGER
LIKE I WAS A STRANGER
ONCE AGAIN
COME ON AND LOVE ME
LIKE I WAS A STRANGER
I WANT TO BE YOUR STRANGER
ONCE AGAIN

(*Return to musical underscoring.*)

    SIX. I'm not a good widow.
I don't want to be.
I'm not going to walk around this town being noble and strong.

A company lets a ship sail in the most dangerous month on the lakes, knowing it needs repairs. For the sake of profits, its minimum freeboard is decreased, so that in 1975 it's carrying several hundred more tons of cargo than was considered safe when it was built.

For their part, the Coast Guard offers a nonfunctioning lighthouse and a rescue ship that is twenty-four hours away.

Reporters stand on my lawn.

When I go out to get the paper, they shove microphones and cameras in my face.

They ask me how it *feels*.

The phone rings late at night and I exchange one nightmare for another.

A man with a soft voice: "Your husband owed me a thousand dollars that he never paid back. You don't want me to spread rumors about him and give him a bad name."

A woman's voice: "Your husband was sleeping with a woman in Detroit. Give me three thousand dollars or I'll tell your kids."

Blackmail and blind rage.

I can't be graceful about that.

I can't watch another flower thrown on the water.

My heart went down with that ship.

(*Return to song. This verse is sung by the SINGER in front of Actor Six.*)

    SINGER TWO.
AND WOULD YOU TOUCH ME
LIKE I WAS A PENNY
LIKE I WAS YOUR MONEY
ONCE AGAIN
COME ON AND LOVE ME
LIKE YOU'D LOVE TO LOVE ME

LIKE YOU WERE ABOVE ME
   ONCE AGAIN

ALL THREE SINGERS.
AND I WANT
I WANT TO BE A RUNE-STONE
DEEP INSIDE YOUR MEMORY
AND I WANT, I WANT TO BE THE MOSS THAT
   GROWS
ON THE NORTH SIDE OF YOUR TREE
ON THE NORTH SIDE
OF YOUR TREE

(*Return to musical underscoring.*)

   FOUR. So, I held his head in my lap and kept him awake.
   He grumbled and bitched.
   I told him all the things about my life that I would change.
   For my benefit he tried to complain about working on the lakes.
   I didn't buy it.
   Sometimes I thought the only way to keep that man home was to toss water on the house and shake it.

   I told him all the things I do when he's gone.
   My little rituals.
   Sometimes his eyes would start to close, so I'd start to lie.
   He'd stay awake to keep me honest.
   He told me his favorite part of the year was Halloween to Thanksgiving.

   I held his head for hours.
   When I had run out of stories and jokes and lies and possible names for all our possible children and pets—he put his finger on my lips.

"Honey I'm fine. Let me sleep."

I remember it as one of my favorite nights.

(*Return to song. This verse is sung by SINGER in front of Actor Four.*)

SINGER THREE.
WOULD YOU LOOK AT ME
LIKE I WAS A STRANGER
LIKE I WAS A STRANGER
ONCE AGAIN
COME ON AND LOVE ME
LIKE I WAS A STRANGER
I WANT TO BE YOUR STRANGER
ONCE AGAIN

(*As the song is concluding, the MEN leave the women, one by one. Song ends.*
LIGHTS reveal the long, narrow table set at a rake, as before. ALL THE MEN, with the exception of ACTOR NINE, are present. The stool downstage of the table is empty. The MEN are eating and drinking, as before. ACTOR SEVEN holds a newspaper. There is a moment of tactile sound, then the conversations erupt.)

ONE. It's like falling asleep.
TWO. How?
ONE. That's what it's like.
TWO. How is it like falling asleep?
ONE. It's like the *sensation* of falling asleep.
TWO. Yeah?
ONE. There's no pain.
SIX. Wish Bishop was here.
FIVE. He's got an ulcer.
SIX. What, and I don't?
FIVE. He couldn't make the trip. Let it go.

EIGHT. What time is it?
FOUR. 7:15.
THREE. I'm having breakfast with my wife this morning. Eggs, cornflakes, English muffin with peanut butter, nothin' special, just *breakfast*—
EIGHT. Anyone seen the cadet?
FOUR. No.
THREE. —and I got a pack of matches from the Chinese Lantern in my shirt pocket.
TWO. I can't believe there's no pain.
THREE. My wife's tellin' me about some movie she wants to see with what's-his-name in it and I'm slappin' peanut butter on my muffin—and the matches in my pocket *ignite*.
ONE. There is a momentary panic.
THREE. The two of us are sitting there, staring at my shirt.
ONE. Then, peace.
THREE. My goddamn shirt is *smoldering*. I rip it off and toss it in the sink. My egg is cold now. I take out the charred matchbook and examine it.
FOUR. I don't get the big deal about fog.
THREE. Every match has burned except one.
FOUR. It's just light. Thick light.
THREE. How would that *happen*? What would ignite it?
FIVE. Aliens.
SIX. Your breath.
THREE. I'm serious.
FIVE. So are we.
SEVEN. I-E or E-I?
ONE. What?
SEVEN. Is it I-E or E-I?
ONE. Me?
SEVEN. The cadet.
ONE. Oh.
THREE. I don't get that.
ONE. E-I.

SEVEN. (*Looking at newspaper.*) Spelled it wrong.
SIX. Bishop and I had some great fights.
FIVE. He didn't make the trip.
SIX. I know that.
FIVE. Let it go.
SIX. I'm just talking.
TWO. You mail your car payment?
ONE. Shit.
TWO. Yeah. Me, too.
SEVEN. This one says we're bound for Gary.
EIGHT. The Anderson was bound for Gary.
SEVEN. Says we were, too.
EIGHT. Toss it.
SIX. It's a joy to fight with someone.
EIGHT. Detroit.
SIX. It's a rush.
EIGHT. Bound for Detroit.
SIX. It reaffirms control.
TWO. This momentary panic?
ONE. Yeah?
TWO. *How* momentary?
ONE. Fleeting. Seductive.
EIGHT. What time is it?
ONE. It courts you.
FOUR. 7:15.
EIGHT. Anyone seen the cadet?
TWO. Okay. Now, *after* the momentary panic.
SIX. It's a gift to get angry.
ONE. Then, peace.
TWO. That's where you lose me.
SIX. It's a joy to push what can be pushed.
ONE. The chemical makeup of hemoglobin is almost identical to that of sea water.
FIVE. We got pie tonight?
THREE. I'm through with pies.
ONE. It is familiar to the body.
SIX. We need the conflict.
FIVE. What is he *saying?*

SIX. The violence we inflict on one another is in direct proportion to the violence nature inflicts on us.

(*Pause.*)

FIVE. Your Chevy still for sale?
SIX. We affect what we can affect.
TWO. Yeah.
SIX. And pray to be spared the rest.
FIVE. Automatic or stick?
FOUR. I was walking in the tunnel tonight—
TWO. Stick.
FOUR. —the tunnel under the spar deck. I was coming to the pilothouse from the rear deckhouse. And I see the door at the other end of the tunnel—five hundred feet away.
SEVEN. Listen to this.
FOUR. And as we fight the storm, the ship begins to *bend*. And I see the door at the far end of the tunnel rise up and out of sight.
TWO. (*Softly.*) Jesus.
SEVEN. Front page. *The New York Times.* 11 November 1975. (*Reads from paper.*) "Ship lost with twenty-nine in Lake Superior. Lifeboats, but no survivors, of ore carrier found—waves twenty feet high."
FOUR. There a picture?
FIVE. An old one.
SEVEN. "Commander Charles Millradt, supervisor of the Coast Guard search, said today that the chances of finding any survivors from the craft, the Edmund Fitzgerald, were, quote, pretty hopeless, unquote."
EIGHT. Time?
FOUR. 7:15.
SEVEN. "'Whenever we get tremendous northwest winds in November,' Commander Millradt said, 'we get a major disaster.'"
EIGHT. Has anyone seen—

(*A MAN (ACTOR NINE) walks to the table, talking. The MEN watch him.*)

MAN WHO WALKS THROUGH SCENES. ... and through the years without knowing it my fear of the pool became my fascination with the pool and years later as I worked on the lakeboats the story would drift back to me and I would remember ...

(*ACTOR NINE is standing at the upstage end of the table. ACTOR SEVEN raises his mug for a toast.*)

SEVEN. Gentlemen, *The New York Times.*

(*ALL THE MEN except ACTOR NINE lift their mugs: tableau. ACTOR NINE speaks to the audience from the head of the table.*

NINE. I am surrounded by water and it is magnificent.
It is within me and without me.
I inhale and it fills me like pure oxygen.
My heart pumps water.
My arteries flood.
I hear waves crash against bone.

I am not frightened.
I do not struggle.
I move with a grace that I am unaccustomed to.
I walk in huge strides toward the horizon.

When I wake, I am breathing air.
And it disappoints me.
The land is so clumsy.
And so shallow.

(*As the MEN hold their tableau, ACTOR NINE moves to the heretofore empty ninth stool at the downstage end of*

the table. HE sits. HE lifts his mug. HE swings his arm forward, the tableau breaks and the mugs come together and clink. The MEN drink.
The toast leads directly into the song: WIDOWS OF THE WATER. LIGHTS go out on the table as the song begins.)

SINGERS.
ALL OF YOUR JACKIES
ALL YOUR JOLLY YOUNG LADDIES
ALL OF YOUR SUMMER
AND WINTER DADDIES FREE
ALL OF YOUR DARING
AND YOUR DASHING YOUNG SKIPPERS
WIDOWS OF THE WATER
WHERE CAN THEY BE?

(MUSIC continues under as LIGHTS reveal COOPER holding the life vest we saw at the end of Act I. An additional LIGHT reveals the YOUNG MAN. HE is holding the sealed jar with the cassette tape in it, as HE did at the beginning of Act I. THEY speak to the audience.)

COOPER. On a beach near Coppermine Point, one additional life vest washed up on 20 April 1976—five months after the Fitzgerald was lost.
The final Casualty Report absolved the company, the Coast Guard and the captain of the Fitzgerald of any and all wrongdoing.
After the search was officially called off, the Coast Guard sent a plane to fly over the area once every hour.
YOUNG MAN.
Water makes many beds
For those averse to sleep—
COOPER. This was amended to once every day.
YOUNG MAN.
Its awful chamber open stands,

Its curtains blandly sweep.
COOPER. Then once a week.
YOUNG MAN.
Abhorrent is the rest
In undulating rooms
COOPER. Then once a month.
YOUNG MAN.
Whose amplitude no end invades,
COOPER. No further action was taken.
YOUNG MAN.
Whose axis never comes.
COOPER. And the case was closed.

(*Return to song. COOPER and the YOUNG MAN are gone. During this part of the song, ALL NINE MEN arrive onstage, one by one. ACTOR FIVE is the first to arrive. The MEN wear black suits and are putting on the finishing touches: tying ties, adjusting sleeves, putting on coats, etc. THEY talk silently, joke and help spruce each other up. THEY end up in positions identical to the ones THEY were in at the beginning of the play, scattered about the bare stage, facing the audience.*)

SINGERS.
ALL OF YOUR SAILING
AND YOUR SALIENT SAILORS
ALL OF YOUR JACKTAR BOYS
AND MARINERS SO FREE
ALL OF THEIR FACES
WITH THEIR BUCKY CHEEKS SO ROSY
WIDOWS OF THE WATER
WHERE CAN THEY BE?

WHERE CAN THEY BE?
AT THE TABLE OF THE WISHES
BREAKING BREAD WITH THE FISHES?
WHERE CAN THEY BE?

TEN NOVEMBER 93

DEVIL-DOGGIN' IN THE WATER
LIKE AN EEL OR AN OTTER?
WHERE CAN THEY BE?
ARE THEY FROLICKING DOWN IN THE WAVES
ON A ROLLICKING SHELLBACK FOOL-AROUND?
ARE THEY LAUGHIN' AS THEY SWIM TO THE
   GRAVE
ALL THEIR JACKETS ON
A LITTLE WATERLOGGED
BUT STILL JUST DEVIL-DOGGIN' DOWN AND
   DOWN AND ON?

(*There is a break in the song. We hear a BELL begin to toll. As the bell tolls, the SINGERS announce the names of the men.*)

SINGER ONE. Ernest M. McSorley. Captain.
SINGER TWO. John H. McCarthy. First Mate.
SINGER THREE. James A. Pratt. Second Mate.
SINGER ONE. Michael E. Armagost. Third Mate.
SINGER TWO. George J. Holl. Chief Engineer.
SINGER THREE. Edward F. Bindon. First Assistant Engineer.
SINGER ONE. Thomas E. Edwards. Second Assistant Engineer.
SINGER TWO. Russell G. Haskell. Second Assistant Engineer.
SINGER THREE. Oliver J. Champeau. Third Assistant Engineer.
SINGER ONE. Frederick J. Beetcher. Porter.
SINGER TWO. Thomas Bentsen. Oiler.
SINGER THREE. Thomas D. Borgeson. Able-bodied Maintenance Man.
SINGER ONE. Nolan F. Church. Porter.
SINGER TWO. Ransom E. Cundy. Watchman.
SINGER THREE. Bruce L. Hudson. Deckhand.
SINGER ONE. Allen G. Kalmon. Second Cook.
SINGER TWO. Gordon F. MacLellan. Wiper.

SINGER THREE. Joseph W. Mazes. Special Maintenance Man.
SINGER ONE. Eugene W. O'Brien. Wheelsman.
SINGER TWO. Karl A. Peckol. Watchman.
SINGER THREE. John J. Poviach. Wheelsman.
SINGER ONE. Robert C. Rafferty. Temporary First Cook.
SINGER TWO. Paul M. Riipa. Deckhand.
SINGER THREE. John D. Simmons. Wheelsman.
SINGER ONE. William J. Spengler. Watchman.
SINGER TWO. Mark A. Thomas. Deckhand.
SINGER THREE. Ralph G. Walton. Oiler
SINGER ONE. David E. Weiss. Cadet.
SINGER TWO. Blaine H. Wilhelm. Oiler.

(*Return to song. The bell stops tolling. Nine pin spots on nine faces.*)

SINGERS.
ALL OF YOUR LOVERS
AND YOUR FATHERS AND YOUR BROTHERS
ALL OF THEM DRIFTING
FROM YOUR MEMORY
OH YOU CAN WEEP OR WONDER
BUT THEY DON'T GIVE A THUNDER
NO THEY DON'T GIVE A GODDAMN
FOR THEY'VE BEEN ALL SET FREE

(*Song ends. Darkness. Silence.*)

END OF PLAY

FAVORITE MUSICALS from
"THE HOUSE OF PLAYS"

BALLROOM – THE BEST LITTLE
WHOREHOUSE IN TEXAS – CHICAGO –
CHRISTMAS IS COMIN' UPTOWN – THE CLUB –
DAMES AT SEA – DIAMOND STUDS –
EL GRANDE DE COCA COLA – GREASE
A HISTORY OF THE AMERICAN FILM – I LOVE
MY WIFE – I'M GETTING MY ACT TOGETHER
AND TAKING IT ON THE ROAD –
LITTLE MARY SUNSHINE – THE ME NOBODY
KNOWS – OF THEE I SING – ON THE
TWENTIETH CENTURY – PETER PAN –
PURLIE – RAISIN – RUNAWAYS – SEESAW –
SHENANDOAH – SOMETHING'S AFOOT –
STRIDER – THEY'RE PLAYING OUR SONG –
THE WIZ

Consult our *Musicals Catalogue* for details.

Other Publications for Your Interest

MAIL
(ADVANCED GROUPS—MUSICAL)
Book & Lyrics by JERRY COLKER
Music by MICHAEL RUPERS

9 men, 6 women—2 Sets

What a terrific idea for a "concept musical"! As *Mail* opens Alex, an unpublished novelist, is having an acute anxiety attack over his lack of success in writing and his indecision regarding his girlfriend, Dana; so, he "hits the ground running" and doesn't come back for 4 months! When Alex finally returns to his apartment, he finds an unending stream of messages on his answering machine and stacks and stacks of unopened mail. As he opens his mail, it in effect comes to life, as we learn what has been happening with Alex's friends, and with Dana, during his absence. There is also some hilarious junk mail, which bombards Alex musically, as well as unpaid bills from the likes of the electric company (the ensemble comes dancing out of Alex's refrigerator singing "We're Gonna Turn Off Your Juice"). In the second act, we move into a sort of abstract vision of Alex's world, a blank piece of paper upon which he can, if he is able, and if he wishes, start over— with his writing, with his friends, with his father and, maybe, with Dana. Producers looking for something wild and crazy will, we know, want to open *this* MAIL, a hit with audiences and critics coast-to-coast, from the authors of THREE GUYS NAKED FROM THE WAIST DOWN! "At least 12 songs are solid enough to stand on their own. If MAIL can't deliver, there is little hope for the future of the musical theatre, unless we continue to rely on the British to take possession of a truly American art form."—Drama-Logue. "Make room for the theatre's newest musical geniuses."—The Same. (Terms quoted on application. Music available on rental. See p. 48.)

(#15199)

CHESS
(ADVANCED GROUPS—MUSICAL/OPERA)
Book by RICHARD NELSON
Lyrics by TIM RICE
Music by BJORN ULVAEUS & BENNY ANDERSSON

9 men, 2 women, 1 female child, plus ensemble

A *musical* about an *international chess match?!?!* A bad idea from the get-go, you'd think; but no—Tim Rice (he of *Evita, Joseph and the Amazing Technicolor Dreamcoat* and *Jesus Christ Superstar*), Bjorn Ulvaeus and Benny Andersson (they of Swedish Supergroup ABBA) and noted American playwright Richard Nelson, all in collaboration with Trevor Nunn (*Les Miz., Nick Nick.* etc.) have pulled it off, creating an extraordinary rock opera about international intrigue which uses as a metaphor a media-drenched chess match between a loutish American champion (shades of Bobby Fischer) and a nice-guy Soviet champion. The American has a girlfriend, Florence, there in Bangkok (where the match takes place) to be his second and to provide moral support. There she meets, and falls in love with, Anatoly, the Soviet champion—and the sparks fly, particularly when Anatoly decides to defect to the west, causing a postponement and change of venue to Budapest. Eventually, it is clear that all the characters are merely pawns in a larger chess match between the C.I.A. and the KGB! The pivotal role of Florence is perhaps the most extraordinary and complex role in the musical theatre since Eva Peron; and the roles of Freddie and Anatoly (both tenors) are great, too. Several of the songs have become international hits, including Florence's "Heaven Help My Heart", "I know Him So Well" and "Nobody's On Nobody's Side", and Freddie's descent into the maelstrom of decadence, "One Night in Bangkok". Playing to full houses and standing ovations, *Chess* closed exceedingly prematurely on Broadway; and, perhaps the story behind *that* just might make the basis of another Rice/ABBA/Nelson/Nunn collaboration! (Terms quoted on application. Music available on rental. See p. 48.) Slightly restricted.

(#5236)